If you're ready for a change in your relationship with God, then *Knowing Grace* will be a helpful guidebook for you to explore a number of spiritual practices that many Christians have used to grow closer to God. First you'll learn about the particular practice from Scripture, next Dr. Jung offers a helpful orientation, and then you'll benefit from brief reflections of those who tried out each practice. Engaging in these practices while opening yourself to God provides a way to live more and more in God's grace.

KLAUS ISSLER
Professor of Christian Education and Theology
Talbot School of Theology, Biola University

Knowing Grace is a helpful, joy-filled, and thoroughly biblical guide to participating with the Holy Spirit in being progressively formed into the image of Jesus. Recommended!

MIKE ERRE
Lead Pastor, Mariners Church, Mission Viejo
Author of *Jesus of Suburbia* and *Why the Bible Matters*

If you're tired of being a lukewarm Christian and want to truly understand who God is, this book is for you! In *Knowing Grace*, Joanne Jung shares with us the ways God would want us to seek him and understand him. She reveals the way truly passionate Christians seek God and why they are able to experience him at a level most believers never get to. You won't find this kind of teaching and Biblical understanding in a regular Sunday service, but then again, you're not looking to be just any ordinary Christian either!

MICHAEL CHANG
1989 French Open Tennis Cham·˙
Biola University Board of Truste

D1489062

Books on the spiritual disciplines are plentiful, and Bible study resources are abundant. To have a book that covers many of the practices Christians should be pursuing and embeds them in a practical and systematic study of God's Word—that is rare. In *Knowing Grace*, Joanne Jung leads us with poetic and practical precision down an elegant path to an outcome all believers should desire for their lives: to truly know the glorious means by which God has saved and is saving us. Whether you are using this book in a small group or in the solitude of your own study, *Knowing Grace* will help you "cultivate a lifestyle of godliness" in your soul.

STAN JANTZ
CEO, ConversantLife.com
Co-author, *God Is in the Small Stuff*

Dr. Jung provides piercing insight on necessary elements of spiritual formation coupled with powerful scriptural precedents that will encourage the growth of any Christ follower.

PASTOR BRYAN LORITTS
Fellowship Memphis

Knowing Grace communicates the access we have to the power God desires to infuse in our lives. Jung speaks in a language we can all understand, making way for the life-giving faith we long to embrace.

STEPHANIE KAIHOI
Founder of Legacy Living Ministries

Delightful, challenging, encouraging, scriptural—this marvelous book is a wise and loving guide toward letting the Spirit stir you to become more like Jesus.

LEE STROBEL
Author of *The Case for the Real Jesus*

Knowing
GRACE

For Woihwan...

May you know, experience, &
enjoy God's grace even
more!

Blessings,
Joan

2 Cor 4:15
2012

Knowing GRACE

Cultivating a Lifestyle of Godliness

Joanne Jung

Transforming lives through God's Word

Transforming lives through God's Word

Biblica provides God's Word to people through translation, publishing and Bible engagement in Africa, Asia Pacific, Europe, Latin America, Middle East, and North America. Through its worldwide reach, Biblica engages people with God's Word so that their lives are transformed through a relationship with Jesus Christ.

Biblica Publishing
We welcome your questions and comments.

1820 Jet Stream Drive, Colorado Springs, CO 80921 USA
www.Biblica.com

Knowing Grace
ISBN-13: 978-1-60657-090-6

A catalog record for this book is available through the Library of Congress.

Printed in the United States of America

CONTENTS

Thank you, God,
for my family, friends, colleagues, and students
whose love, encouragement, and prayers
have been and continue to be conduits of your grace to me.
May each reader be blessed in similar ways.

HOW TO USE
THIS BOOK

You could read through this book and begin to incorporate these rhythms in your life without reading this page, but you may miss the intent woven throughout the following chapters. Though each self-contained chapter focuses on a means of grace, there is an intentional sequence to the whole. The hope for optimal spiritual transformation orchestrated by God will involve engagement with his Word. "Getting into the Word" and "The Word Getting into Us" form that foundation. The next few means ("Silence and Solitude," "Fasting," and "Prayer") are designed to heighten your ability to reduce the desensitizing distractions that interfere with knowing, recognizing, and becoming more frequently drawn into the presence of God. As you grow in understanding of the condition of your heart, you will be better able to sense the grace God extends to believers through "Confession," "Conference," and even "Suffering." "Biblical Hospitality," "Biblical Thanksgiving," and "Service" will alert you to the outward opportunities that reflect your growing sensitivity to God's Spirit. Living "Celebration" actualizes the foretaste of your participation in the culmination of human history.

The following questions—based on the chapter divisions—are designed to foster reflection and to facilitate community through

dialogue. Though useful for personal contemplation, these questions draw participants in small groups toward caring for each other's soul.

- Which word or words found in the **Definition** of the means of grace were the most meaningful to you? Why?
- Explore further one of the passages from the Old or New Testament in the **Letting the Word Speak** section. How do the surrounding texts add even more depth to your understanding of the passage cited?
- As you read through the **Food for Thought** of each means, what personal thoughts came to mind?
- Could you identify with any of the **Pitfalls** in the chapter? How? Is there a pitfall that you would add?
- Did the words in the **God's Stirring** section serve to encourage you, or did you feel a bit of fear?
- After having read and practiced a means of grace, did you resonate with any of the reflections? Which one? How? Try writing your own **Reflection** on your experience, and share it with a friend.
- Which friend can you tell how you completed the **Fill in the Blank** sentence?
- What would be your own **Closing Thought**?
- If you read a selection from the **Helpful Reads**, what additional help was offered?

There are no right or wrong answers. Sharing your reflections with others will cultivate the kind of community where people grow closer to God and to one another.

INTRODUCTION
STIRRED CHOCOLATE MILK

Grace. You've heard it defined as "God's riches at Christ's expense" or as "unmerited favor." These are a good start. More fully, grace is the way God has chosen to act toward creation and, specifically, toward all humankind. God's gift of his Son, Jesus Christ, is the ultimate expression of grace extended to undeserving people. The gift of the Holy Spirit, who takes the things of God and presents them to the soul, also enables believers to live transformed lives. This is yet another expression of God's grace. God's changelessness means that this is the way he will always communicate his kind disposition and transforming power toward us. Our growth in godliness, or Christlikeness, then is critically dependent on God's grace, learning to respond to the initiations of God. And all of this is appropriated by grace through faith.

There is no season of life exempt from God's wanting to grow our faith and our understanding of grace. Sometimes his stirring presents itself in the form of questions. Here are two that seem to persist for us: Who am I? and, How do I make my faith my own?

The question of your identity isn't answered by what you do or what roles you fill. Do you limit your identity to a job, bank account, car, or house? Do you think of yourself as a parent or a coach—or as who you say you are on the Internet? Do you define

yourself from advertisements, song lyrics, movies, the mirror, or your blog?

God said that we were all created in his image. This image was present in the first human beings and is still present in us. With the fall of Adam, that image survived but was marred. Evidence of that image is in you. Because you were made in the image of God, you are inextricably related to who God is.

The second question is related to the first. Whether you are new to the Christian faith or have grown up in a Christian environment, you will face this question: How do I make my faith my own? It's uncomfortable riding the coattails of parents, pastors, or some idolized heroes of the faith. If we are impressed by the mature faith of godly models around us, it may cause us to wonder how we could ever have that kind of giant-sized faith, considering our inconsistencies and irregularities. A lot of people have these thoughts and want to know, What is *my* own faith supposed to be like?

If you wrestle with answering these questions, the concepts involved in spiritual formation will greatly assist you. Spiritual formation means allowing the truth of who God is and how he sees you to transform you. Spiritual formation provides the course by which we as individuals in community grow in grace and truth and marks our personal journey of faith as unique and genuine.

Defining Spiritual Formation

Libraries and Internet sites abound with definitions for spiritual formation. Before we go any further, let's take a look at a few of God's words. After all, if he plans, provides, and performs our transformation, surely his Word must speak of it. Here are some passages that reveal his involvement:

- **Philippians 2:12–13:** "Therefore, my beloved, as you have always obeyed, so now, not only as in my presence but much more in my absence, work out your own salvation with fear and trembling, for it is God who works in you, both to will and to work for his good pleasure." In these verses we see that God esteems us enough to invite us to join him in his work of our transformation.

- **1 Corinthians 15:10:** "But by the grace of God I am what I am, and his grace toward me was not in vain. On the contrary, I worked harder than any of them, though it was not I, but the grace of God that is with me." God's grace is in believers and it manifests to others.
- **2 Corinthians 9:8:** "And God is able to make all grace abound to you, so that having all sufficiency in all things at all times, you may abound in every good work." God's grace is available to us for our every need.
- **2 Peter 3:18:** "But grow in the grace and knowledge of our Lord and Savior Jesus Christ. To him be the glory both now and to the day of eternity. Amen." We are to grow and keep growing in the wonder-filled grace and the transforming knowledge of Christ.

A number of definitions of spiritual formation have been written over the years. Jeffrey Greenman, associate dean of biblical and theological studies at Wheaton College, collaborated with others to define it in this way: "Spiritual formation is the continuing response to the reality of God's grace shaping us into the likeness of Jesus Christ, through the work of the Holy Spirit, in the community of faith for the sake of the world."[1] This definition highlights the process of God's initiation and our response, community involvement, and the purpose. It also acknowledges the Trinity: God's grace, Christlikeness, and the working of the Holy Spirit.

Often spiritual formation is equated with the spiritual disciplines. There is a temptation to think of spiritual formation as the result of a formula—that if I just do certain activities, I'll be mature. Frustration can set in, however, when we don't see any immediate change. We must remember, however, that our spiritual formation is a lifelong process and that we are not alone in it.

Indeed, each of the members of the Trinity plays a part.

The Father, Son, and Holy Spirit have roles, functions, and power in designing, modeling, and empowering us in this endeavor of receiving and allowing God's grace to grow and strengthen our faith. God is constantly extending his grace to us. He invites us to come to him, spend time with him, and become like him. His goal is to make us like Christ. The power to accomplish this is the abiding presence of his Spirit. When we understand that almighty God is at work in us for our spiritual formation, we may feel that a huge weight has been lifted from us.

Psalm 139:7

Our part in this process is to respond to God, who is always working toward our transformation. Our individual responses take place in community. Spiritual formation has always been a communal activity, but our society's hyperindividualistic and isolationistic trends for personal success contradict the rhythms of spiritual growth. However, as children of God we have received an incomparable helper and gift—the Holy Spirit has taken up residence in us. Christ's Spirit now lives in us, transforming our lives to be living, breathing signposts, pointing others to God.

A Glass of Milk

Imagine our lives before coming to saving faith in Christ as a clear glass filled with plain milk. At a point in time, we came to the realization that we needed a Savior, Christ. We prayed the sinner's prayer, received forgiveness, and immediately became members of God's family. At that moment, we were given the gift of the Holy Spirit. Pouring a generous amount of Hershey's chocolate syrup into the glass of milk pictures the fullness of the Holy Spirit given to us. Stirring the mixture with a spoon ensures the smooth blending of the chocolate syrup and milk. The stirring illustrates our involvement (or continued involvement) in such things as church, prayer, Bible study, worship, and service toward others. What is the intended outcome? Not just chocolate in milk, but thoroughly stirred chocolate milk. That's what we are designed

to become: people who evidence the working—stirring—of the Holy Spirit as he mediates Jesus Christ in our lives. Jesus continues to work in us and teach us by his Holy Spirit, maturing our belief in who God is and what he wants to do.

Imagine another glass of plain milk. This time, though, the chocolate syrup and spoon are actionless. The syrup clearly settles at the bottom of the glass. Now compare the two glasses. Both illustrate the reality of a believer, but only one pictures a life that is growing in godliness, actualizing genuine spiritual transformation. The other illustrates the life of someone whose growth is stunted and who shows little evidence of being a true believer.

We must be careful that we are not depending on our own power to transform ourselves. This is a pseudotransformation because it is not emanating from the Holy Spirit. J. I. Packer drew on a thought from English Puritan John Owen and put it this way: "One may be capable of performances that benefit others spiritually and yet be a stranger oneself to the Spirit-wrought inner transformation that true knowledge of God brings. The manifestation of the Spirit in charismatic performance is not the same thing as the fruit of the Spirit in Christlike character, and there may be much of the former with little or none of the latter."[2] Living the façade of the Christian life is tiring; pseudotransformation is far from the sustainable life of impact for which were we created.

Do you know anyone who is like this glass of unstirred chocolate milk? These are people whose lifestyle shows little or no evidence of the Spirit's power or prompting. Perhaps we don't even have to go as far as asking whether we know someone who lives like this because we are the ones lacking the evidence of God growing us into the image of his Son. C. S. Lewis, in *Mere Christianity*, put it this way: "The real Son of God is at your side. He is beginning to turn you into the same kind of thing as Himself. He is beginning, so to speak, to 'inject' His kind of life and thought, His *Zoe* [life], into you; beginning to turn the tin soldier into a live man. The part of you that does not like it is the part that is still tin."[3]

The purpose of this book is to help you turn tin into tinder, producing a heart that burns consistently and steadily, like—and for—God's heart. This kind of heart reveals a growing knowledge of and dependence on God and, in so doing, it is a heart that reveals truly who you are.

God, in his commitment to transform us, continues to extend his grace in providing various means to stir us. A seventeenth-century saint of old, John Preston, said this about means of grace: "You must take heed of depending upon the meanes without GOD. For know that the meanes without God, is but as a penne without Inke, a Pipe without water, or a scabbard without a sword. They will not strengthen the inward man without God: for it is the Spirit that puts life in the meanes, . . . so the meanes are as pipes to carry grace into the soule."[4]

Romans
9:14-16

It is by grace we were called into God's family. It is by grace we grow in truth, knowledge, and love in that family. Our journey of experiencing God's commitment to transform us more and more into the likeness of Christ began with his grace and will continue by means of that same grace. Our spiritual formation requires a lifestyle of knowing and responding to this deep and far-reaching grace.

The Spoon

Returning to our image of the two glasses of milk, what does the spoon represent? Obviously, in the unstirred chocolate milk, it is positioned there, but its lack of motion has no apparent effect. In the glass of stirred milk, the spoon serves as a valuable instrument. The spoon pictures the various means of grace. Some might call them spiritual disciplines—and they would be correct—but the emphasis in grace is on the actions of the Father, Son, and Holy Spirit in transforming us. We are invited to *engage with* God's Spirit as he changes us as we *engage in* God-given means for our transformation. The more we are changed, the more we long to be changed. Is this challenging? Indeed.

Have you ever been to the Great Wall of China? It is named as one of the new seven wonders of the world. Standing on this wall, you are struck by its history, longevity, and sheer mass, and by the splendor of the surrounding terrain. To walk any of the 5,164 steps is enough to tax even the fittest—not simply because of the number of steps but because the rutted steps are quite irregular, varying in height, depth, and width. Perhaps used as part of a defense strategy, the steps posed quite a training exercise for those stationed anywhere along the wall. The steps never changed, but the abilities of those who walked them day after day did change. Their nimbleness became an advantage over any encroaching enemy, enabling them to navigate the wall with skill and agility.

Incorporating the means of grace in our lives has similar effects. These may feel uncomfortable at first, but think about this: God esteems us by his invitation to participate with him in the process of spiritual transformation. Under the direction, guidance, and power of the Trinity, and with our cooperation, these means can be particularly helpful in our walk with God. We become more attentive to God's stirring in our souls while plumbing the spiritual depths in becoming who we are intended to be.

The Intended Outcome

We must not allow the *means* to become *ends* in themselves. We are not called to become Captain Solitude or Fasting Queen, or to see who can fast or meditate the longest. We are designed to be stirred chocolate milk. Because God is love, our spiritual formation will be about loving him and loving others. Fortunately, there is no SFAT (Spiritual Formation Aptitude Test) to constantly assess this growth. Yet, there are two questions that reflect the vertical and horizontal dimensions of the love God desires us to have. They are taken from Matthew 22: 37–39: Is my love for God increasing? and, Is my love for people increasing?

If we are completely truthful about ourselves, there are times when we must answer "No" to these questions. When that

happens, we have likely let the diverting influences of the world and our unrelenting self-centeredness seep into that which directs our lives—our hearts. Because the heart houses the mind, emotion, and will, God knows how critical it is for us to pay attention to it, for from the heart flow the issues of life. If any transformation is going to take place, it must first be a matter of the heart. Our lives, then, become our hearts in motion. God will have reached his intended purpose in us when we find ourselves loving him and others more deeply and intentionally.

God uses the means of grace to cultivate our familiarity with his movements and voice. In conjunction with his written Word, by his Spirit, our hearts become more prone to recognize his presence in our lives and better able to recognize the obstacles that thwart our obedience. Progressively, over time, we grow in godliness.

The means of grace that are included in this book are grounded in Scripture and have been found to be helpful and of great benefit to Christians throughout history. Each chapter houses a number of key elements. First, there is a definition of the means of grace to be discussed. This will focus our attention on God's perspective of each means. The definition is followed by a section called **Letting the Word Speak**. Here supporting biblical passages from the Old and New Testaments are presented with a brief comment on each. It is recommended that the reader explore the surrounding texts, as space has limited what can be included here.

The **Food for Thought** section offers either a didactic or narrative perspective. The brief How To section describes the approach, whereas the **Pitfalls** segment alerts us to what might get in the way. The **God's Stirring** component allows us to peek at the ways God works in and through these means. The **Reflections from the Heart** are glimpses of the life transformations of other people. After taking an opportunity to exercise a means of grace, add your own reflection in the **Fill in the Blank**

sentence. The **Closing Thought** offers a summarizing conclusion to the time spent in each chapter. The final section, called **Helpful Reads**, suggests books that I have found helpful on the topic of the chapter.

May you grow more familiar with God's movements in your life as his grace and mercy become more deeply known. Enjoy mindfully walking in the company of God.

Knowing Grace

1
GETTING INTO
THE WORD

Definition: God wants to be known, and he accomplishes this primarily through his Word and his Son. God is present in the mind-engaging, heart-affecting, life-impacting reading and study of the Scriptures. If you walk away from reading his Word relating better to him and to others, you have read it correctly.

Letting the Word Speak

Old Testament

Deuteronomy 17:18–20:

> And when he sits on the throne of his kingdom, he shall write for himself in a book a copy of this law, approved by the Levitical priests. And it shall be with him, and he shall read in it all the days of his life, that he may learn to fear the LORD his God by keeping all the words of this law and these statutes, and doing them, that his heart may not be lifted up above his brothers, and that he may not turn aside from the commandment, either to the right hand or to the left, so that he may continue long in his kingdom, he and his children, in Israel.

This passage records the requirements for the kings who would rule Israel. One indisputable obligation was to study and keep the Torah—the first five books of the Old Testament. Knowing and applying God's Word is a must for any godly leader.

2 Chronicles 34:18–19, 30:

> Then Shaphan the secretary told the king, "Hilkiah the priest has given me a book." And Shaphan read from it before the king.
>
> And when the king heard the words of the Law, he tore his clothes.
>
> . . . And the king went up to the house of the LORD, with all the men of Judah and the inhabitants of Jerusalem and the priests and the Levites, all the people both great and small. And he read in their hearing all the words of the Book of the Covenant that had been found in the house of the LORD.

Here we see the people of Israel in a time of crisis. Either they were returning from exile and were puzzled about their identity, or they were coming back to God from a time of spiritual exile. The people were being called back to their God, and the identity of that generation was being redefined. These words reminded them of their beginnings and their continued existence and obligations within a covenant relationship with Yahweh.

Psalm 19:7: "The law of the LORD is perfect, reviving the soul; the testimony of the LORD is sure, making wise the simple."

C. S. Lewis wrote of Psalm 19, "I take this to be the greatest poem in the Psalter and one of the greatest lyrics in the world."[1]

This one verse pivots the reader from God's general revelation found throughout nature and the universe to his special revelation found in his Word, the Bible. Both speak of God. Here the psalmist would be referring to the Torah, and because the Torah reflects God, it can be trusted as the firm foundation of human

life. Anyone lacking sufficient experience to navigate through life's twists and turns will find God's Word critical to know and follow.

Psalm 119:130–131: "The unfolding of your words gives light; it imparts understanding to the simple. I open my mouth and pant, because I long for your commandments."

Each one of the 176 verses that form this psalm expresses the joy of having and knowing God's Word. Wisdom for the "simple," or inexperienced, is among the benefits of understanding and obeying God's Word. The psalmist's appetite for and anticipation of God's Word is met with satisfaction and refreshment.

Jeremiah 15:16: "Your words were found, and I ate them, and your words became to me a joy and the delight of my heart, for I am called by your name, O Lord, God of hosts."

Every day was a challenge for Jeremiah. It was God's call that Jeremiah would represent God's Word to the people, but he was consistently met with cruel and stinging reproach. Yet against the despair and rejection, Jeremiah found joy in taking the Lord's words into his life.

New Testament

Matthew 22:29: "But Jesus answered them, 'You are wrong, because you know neither the Scriptures nor the power of God.'"

The Sadducees accepted only the Pentateuch (or Torah, the first five books of the Old Testament) and denied angelic spirits and bodily resurrection. Their close association with the political, religious, and cultural elite led to a compromise in their theology, which was further compounded by their deficient knowledge of the Scriptures and God's power.

Luke 24:45: "Then he opened their minds to understand the Scriptures."

In this postresurrection appearance, Jesus granted under-

standing of God's message in the Scriptures to the disciples. Luke recorded their earlier blindness in Luke 9:45 and 18:34. The disciples were then able to understand Jesus as the fulfillment of Old Testament messianic prophecies.

John 14:26: "But the Helper, the Holy Spirit, whom the Father will send in my name, he will teach you all things and bring to your remembrance all that I have said to you."

The Holy Spirit reminded the first disciples of Jesus' teaching in light of the significance of his resurrection. This was imperative because of the disciples' responsibility in writing the words of Scripture. As the Son reveals the Father, the Spirit reveals the Christ of history to his followers.

John 15:7: "If you abide in me, and my words abide in you, ask whatever you wish, and it will be done for you."

The word *abide* appears eleven times in seventeen verses here. A critical part of abiding is allowing God's Word to have influence in how we think and live out what we know. There is a relationship between having God's Word in our hearts and prayer. Our transformed thinking allows us to echo the concerns that God has and then to pray for them.

John 16:13: "When the Spirit of truth comes, he will guide you into all the truth, for he will not speak on his own authority, but whatever he hears he will speak, and he will declare to you the things that are to come."

Just as Jesus could do or say only what the Father wanted in order to reveal the Father, the Spirit is dependent on Jesus for everything he says, revealing the unity of God and the glory of Christ. God promises his help in the study of his Word.

Acts 17:11: "Now these Jews were more noble than those in Thessalonica; they received the word with all eagerness, examining the Scriptures daily to see if these things were so."

Paul was pleasantly surprised by the Berean (present-day

Verria) Jews as they welcomed the gospel with a humble receptivity. Many believed; among them were Jews and God-fearing Greeks and men and women belonging to leading families in the city. Their reputation for studying the Word of God set the bar for generations to come. They were enthusiastic to hear from God and respond to what they heard. This kind of "examining" referred to the "cross-examining" or "testing" found in the legal process. As they applied this to the Scriptures, the Bereans sought to prove Paul's assertion that Israel's messianic hope was found in the death and resurrection of Jesus. They refused to be gullible or unthinking in their approach to the Scriptures.

Romans 15:4: "For whatever was written in former days was written for our instruction, that through endurance and through the encouragement of the Scriptures we might have hope."

Paul frequently appealed to the purpose of Scripture. Although the Old Testament was written in the past, it has a teaching purpose in the present. The Old Testament, with its fulfillment found in Christ and the church, fosters hope in suffering and strengthens unity.

1 Corinthians 2:9–12: "But, as it is written, 'What no eye has seen, nor ear heard, nor the heart of man imagined, what God has prepared for those who love him'—these things God has revealed to us through the Spirit. For the Spirit searches everything, even the depths of God. For who knows a person's thoughts except the spirit of that person, which is in him? So also no one comprehends the thoughts of God except the Spirit of God. Now we have received not the spirit of the world, but the Spirit who is from God, that we might understand the things freely given us by God."

Christians can know God's thoughts only to the extent that the Spirit reveals them. Sight, hearing, and intuition are not enough to understand the heart of God. The message of the cross can be understood only by the gracious enabling of the Holy Spirit.

Philippians 1:9–11: "And it is my prayer that your love may abound more and more, with knowledge and all discernment, so that you may approve what is excellent, and so be pure and blameless for the day of Christ, filled with the fruit of righteousness that comes through Jesus Christ, to the glory and praise of God."

Increasing growth in the love of God is reflected in the discernment needed to make the best or "excellent" decisions in a field of many options. This will require a deepened yearning for and engagement with God in his Word.

Colossians 3:16: "Let the word of Christ dwell in you richly, teaching and admonishing one another in all wisdom, singing psalms and hymns and spiritual songs, with thankfulness in your hearts to God."

The receptivity of the Colossians for the word of truth or gospel was apparent from the time Epaphras first preached it to them. To "dwell" was understood as something being the master of the house, not a visiting guest. To "dwell richly" or "abundantly" describes the Word as an inexhaustible spiritual resource that would have its impact on the way believers lived. The corporate context of this passage attests to the mutual responsibility to and for each other in a forgiving, loving, and thankful community.

1 Timothy 4:13: "Until I come, devote yourself to the public reading of Scripture, to exhortation, to teaching."

The first of three ministry commands Paul gave Timothy is for "the public reading of Scripture." This practice was inherited from temple and synagogue worship where the Old Testament was read. The reading of Scripture laid the foundation for the preaching and teaching that followed. God's Word influences the formation, shaping, defining, and redefining of our individual and corporate identity.

2 Timothy 2:15: "Do your best to present yourself to God

as one approved, a worker who has no need to be ashamed, rightly handling the word of truth."

Paul had just warned Timothy what to avoid and then addressed what he was to do. Because conversion is essentially understanding and accepting the gospel as truth, Timothy bore the responsibility, as a representative of the gospel and ambassador of this truth, to teach it correctly.

Food for Thought

If you've ever stood on a mountaintop, looking up in awe at a starlit sky or have been mesmerized by the waxing and waning of the waves at the beach, thoughts of God's power, creativity, beauty, and order have most likely come to mind. Creation gives us "general revelation" of some of God's attributes. But only in God's Word will we find "special revelation," that is, where God most clearly discloses himself and his redemptive plan centered around Jesus.

Often when people study the Bible, they are asked, "What does it mean to you?" This erroneously implies that there is a different meaning for everyone. A distinction should be made here between *meaning* and *significance*. A number of guidelines must be considered to determine the limited meaning of a biblical text; whereas, the implication, application, or significance of that text, though still related to its meaning, needs to be appropriately individualized.

Interpreting a passage requires a bit of investigative work; this is called *hermeneutics*. Sound hermeneutics requires an understanding of the historical context—the culture of the day, the religious atmosphere, Israel's fidelity (or infidelity, as was most often the case), and the intended audience. In addition, the literary context addresses issues about the author—the genre he chose to write in, the big idea of a passage or paragraph, and the use of particular words.

Here's a fun example. Try completing the sentence "Mary

had a little lamb . . ." An expected response might be "its fleece was white as snow." But that would be quite different from the intended thought of "Mary had a little lamb with her peas and carrots." The meaning of a word is found in how it is used in a sentence; the meaning of a sentence is found in how it is used in a paragraph. Together the literary and historical contexts of a passage clarify our understanding of a biblical passage and bring us closer to what God wants to communicate to us through his Word.

The diagram below shows how these elements of hermeneutics come together as we read, understand, and apply Scripture to our lives. The top half displays how we get into the Word, as we interact with the text and helpful sources that enlarge our

Reading the Biblical Text

Historical Context
    Cultural
    Social
    Religious

Literary Context
    Authorial intent
    Intended application
    Expected response
    Genre
    Big idea of the passage
    Paragraph
    Sentence
    Word

Meaning

Contemporary Context
    Cultural
    Social
    Religious

Lectio Divina
    Lectio (Reading)
    Meditatio (Meditation)
    Oratio (Prayer)
    Contemplatio (Contemplation)

Significance
(Implication from God's perspective
informing your specific response)

understanding of Scripture. The bottom half shows how the Word gets into us. Both are required for impactful spiritual transformation. Being able to cite strong support for an interpretation of a passage without allowing God to infuse the truth from his Word into our hearts leaves us with plenty of head knowledge but no living evidence of the transforming power of God. It's like putting on prescription glasses and then walking where there is no light. We may be well equipped, but tragic results are likely.

Without these glasses though, even with the lights on, there will be only blurred images of what is real. It is dangerous to apply a misinterpretation of the Word. Asking only, "What does it mean to *me*?" leads to an interpretive individualism that God never intended for readers of his Word.

Informational reading (which accesses scholarly insights to expand our understanding of the text) together with formational reading (which allows the Word to dwell richly in our hearts) transforms us spiritually into the likeness of Christ. We need both the insights offered by excellent scholars and the power of the Spirit to make God's words effective in our hearts and lives. "Trans[in]formational" reading of the Bible affirms this process: it's not either/or, but a both/and proposition. As we progress in holiness, our faith grows in the knowledge and assurance of God's profound and personal love for us and others.

A key to plumbing the depths of God's Word is the ability to understand the genre of a particular passage. Each of the various genres of Scripture has unique characteristics and requires us to look through a different lens to be able to clearly focus on what God is showing us in a passage.

Confusing the genres can cause misunderstandings. Take for instance this case of mistaken genre. *The War of the Worlds* was a radio drama episode performed on October 30, 1938. Listeners were spellbound as a Martian army invasion of New York City

was broadcast over the airwaves. Others, catching only a segment of the program and missing the repeated notices that the broadcast was fictional, understood this to be a credible newscast and panicked, with many fleeing the area. Applying genres correctly may not save the world, but it will make a world of difference in our ability to read and understand God's Word.

Genre-based hermeneutics, identifying the specific genre as we interpret a portion of Scripture, helps us to arrive at an accurate meaning. Knowing some basic characteristics and beneficial approaches to these nine genres will help us get into the Word.

Old Testament Narratives

Most of the Old Testament is written in narrative or story form, so being able to understand how to explore a story in Scripture is critical. A story is meant to be read as a whole, so try to read larger portions, sometimes ignoring the chapter divisions as these can imply a stop where none was intended. Know also that there are three levels of interpreting an Old Testament story. The highest level involves God revealing who he is and what he is doing in his overall plan of redemption in the world. The middle level shows us how God interacts with his people in a specific historical context. The lowest level, and often a default one, focuses on the main character of the story as a model for how we are to live. The lowest level is not a bad level, but if that level is our only focus, we will have missed not only what God intended to reveal to us through the other two levels but also how God is the real hero of all the stories.

The Law

The first five books of the Old Testament—Genesis, Exodus, Leviticus, Numbers, and Deuteronomy—are known by several names, such as the Torah, the Pentateuch, and the books of the Law. These books contain the many laws that God gave to the nation of Israel when he redeemed his people from Egypt (for example, the Ten Commandments). This law was seen as a gracious

gift from God, a thing of beauty that guided the Israelites and lighted their paths. Beyond the legislative aspect, the law had an instructional purpose, as seen in the 176 verses of Psalm 119, which focuses on the psalmist's devotion to the law and to the Lord.

The law regulated every aspect of life, and the Israelites' obedience to the law distinguished them from every other nation on earth. It was through the law that their relationship with God was established, because the law reveals the heart of the Lawgiver and what is important to him. He is shown to be holy, loving, and intimately concerned with our relationship with him and with each other. So, that same law that was regulatory for the Israelites is revelatory for us now.

The Psalms

Poetry has always had this advantage over prose: the ability for the reader to enter into the imagery and experience of the poet's penned words. A variety of Hebrew poets, over a period of nine hundred years, contributed to the collection called the Psalms. David wrote about 73 of the 150 psalms, and other authors include Moses, Solomon, Heman, Ethan, the families of Asaph and of Korah, and others whose names remain unknown.

Hebrew poetry has some distinguishing marks. Each of these psalms unites human emotion and experience with sound theology and needs to be read as a whole in order to glean the full, developed message the psalmist intended. Many of the psalms were sung to the accompaniment of musical instruments in the worship services of ancient Israel. It is also important to know that there are different types of psalms. They can be hymns of praise, trust, lament, thanksgiving, or wisdom, for instance. This variety dictates that they will convey different ideas. A final characteristic in the psalms is the use of parallelisms. Whereas we are familiar with poetry that rhymes words, Hebrew poetry often rhymes thoughts: two lines are read in connection with each other.

Old Testament Wisdom Literature

The root meaning of the word *wisdom* is "skill." For the Israelites, wisdom was the skill of doing life in the fear of Yahweh (Proverbs 1:7; 9:10). Its overarching purpose was to develop godly character in and through the usual, as well as the challenging, events of life. It is fitting then that some passages in this genre are easy to grasp and understand, while others are quite bewildering. Simple wisdom is characterized by the belief that if you are righteous, you will succeed. Likewise, when you sin, suffering will result. The book of Proverbs is an example of simple wisdom. It is a collection of a few different authors proffering general nuggets of wisdom, or guidelines for successful living. These are not guarantees from God or universal truths for all time and were not intended to be taken as promises from God.

But the whole of life cannot be characterized by simple wisdom. We've all experienced when "good things happen to bad people" and, what is even more puzzling, "when bad things happen to good people." Examples of complex wisdom appear in Job, Ecclesiastes, and Song of Solomon. Job's friends, though commended for sitting with Job in silence for seven days, then proceeded to try to fix Job's reality of suffering by imposing their flawed theology. They found that their "simple wisdom" didn't fit into a situation of "complex wisdom." Job asked the logical question, "Why?" but God was silent until the end of the book. God never did answer Job's question, but Job walked away with far more knowledge of God's sovereignty, power, and care over his creation than if God had simply answered Job's question. Discover the way God discloses his trustworthiness in the Wisdom Literature.

The Prophets

The books of the writing prophets are often overlooked for Bible reading and study. This is a great loss because there is a beautiful richness found in these books. To understand prophetic literature,

we must have knowledge of the historical context. The prophets appeared in a time in Israel's history when the people turned their backs to God. These spokesmen of God warned the divided kingdoms of Israel and Judah of coming judgment if there was no repentance. Whereas in the Law we see God's design for our relationship with him and others, the Prophets show us what happens when these relationships are broken.

The books of the Prophets record the break Israel and Judah made from God that resulted in their worshiping other gods: idolatry. The break in their relationships with one another resulted in rampant social injustices. The *foretelling* by the prophets was focused on the future of Israel, Judah, and other nations. Most of that is history for us now, but their *forthtelling*—proclamations of God's truths, concerns, ways, and will—reveals that the sin of social injustice is no less a sin than idolatry. God's heart for his people and for the poor and disadvantaged is revealed through the prophets, and we learn that he delights when his people grow to have the same heart.

The Gospels

If you want to know what Jesus Christ and his kingdom are like, read the Gospels. There are four of them, and each is the "good news" written to a different audience. Each Gospel has the primary goal of proving that Jesus is the Messiah, the Anointed One, the One sent from God. Because the Gospels are narratives, the historical and cultural background information is important. While it is helpful at times to compare the perspectives a particular Gospel has to another, it is also important to keep the cohesiveness of each Gospel intact so as to understand the author's unique emphasis as he intentionally places the events or themes of Jesus' life in a particular sequence. One of the best ways to read from the Gospels is to imagine yourself in the scene. Imagine being in that crowd as you hear Jesus' teaching on the kingdom, or being the object of a miraculous healing, or even being one of the

Pharisees. As his disciple learning more of him, his message, and his ways, reading the Gospels will reveal the radical purpose, love, and service of the King that is to be characteristic of his kingdom citizens.

Acts

The Acts of the Apostles is often referred to as "the Acts of the Holy Spirit," for surely he is clearly featured as the driving force behind the birth, growth, and expansion of the church. Acts 1:8 organizes the whole of Luke's record of the church: Jerusalem, Judea, and the ends of the earth. At issue is whether the events recorded here are to be *descriptive* (describing the happenings of the early church as it moved from a local to a global position)or to view the events as *prescriptive* (a model for the church to follow today).

Keep in mind the broad picture of Acts. Repeated themes will signal not only Luke's emphases but also those things that may be considered normative for the twenty-first-century church, such as the Spirit's ministry, God's sovereignty, the loving community of the church, prayer, suffering, breaking racial and cultural barriers, and the power of witness. Various characters in this narrative provide godly models to imitate or to allow as mentors. The ungodly behavior of some characters serves as cautionary deterrents. The birth and growth of the early church was not a cakewalk. Our accurate interpretation of this record of the Holy Spirit's movements can only foster a greater appreciation and expectation of his work today.

The Epistles

To say that the Epistles are *occasional* doesn't mean that they were written randomly or every so often. *Occasional* in this sense means that each was written with a specific occasion in mind: behaviors needing correction, doctrinal errors needing to be set right, or misunderstandings requiring further illumination. Because a specific situation is being addressed, knowing background information is

important. As with letters (or e-mails) received in today's world, read the whole epistle in one sitting in order to follow the flow of the author's argument. It won't take you as long as you think. These letters followed the format typical of first-century letters and include three parts: introduction; the body of the letter, where the author addresses issues facing the church; and a conclusion with a final greeting. Paragraphs are the main units of thought, so resist focusing on only one or two verses without looking at the greater whole. The Epistles can enrich our understanding of community for the twenty-first-century church, especially as they inform our identity in Christ, which is individually applied and communally affirmed.

Revelation

The genre of Revelation is actually made up of three genres, two of which have already been introduced: the *occasional* element of an epistle is joined with the *foretelling* aspect of prophecy. Add to these two the third element of apocalyptic literature. Born in times of persecution, apocalyptic literature looks forward to a time of a violent and radical end to history, the triumph of good, and the final judgment of evil.

As easy as it is to focus on the visions described, remember that this book is ultimately about the victor, Jesus Christ, not Satan or the Antichrist. Knowing God's future triumph through Christ is meant to prompt godly choices in holy living in the present. Revelation is filled with over three hundred allusions to the Old Testament; therefore, it is really intended to function as the capstone of all of Scripture and to complete the picture of what God has been doing in human history. John expected his readers to hear his echoes of the Old Testament as the continuation—and consummation—of that story. Twenty-first-century readers would be wise to do the same.

How To

God is present when we open his Word and search the Scriptures, so it makes sense to prayerfully ask the God of the Word into our study. It is his desire that we who bear his image would have his Word in our hearts, from which every attitude, action, and spoken word flows. As his Spirit gives illumination and understanding to the intake of the truth, he then gives expression of that truth.

Sharpening our understanding of the genres and examining Scripture through correct lenses foster a more accurate interpretation of the Word. Before you choose a passage to read, review the characteristics and principles unique to the genre in which that passage is found. As you apply these simple guidelines, God will enlarge your understanding of him through his Word.

Pitfalls

Busyness

One of the most common reasons given for people not reading the Bible is busyness. Our world is saturated with things to do, places to go, and people to see—or at least Facebook. A closer look into this reason brings up the question, Why have we allowed our schedules to consume and direct so much of our lives, creating a low priority for connecting with God through his Word?

This inflated view of self corresponds to a deflated view of God, resulting in him becoming the servant whose purpose is to tend to our needs. Our view of God will be proportional to our receptivity to his Word. The words of a little God will have limited power and influence. The self-revealing words of a perfect, holy, all-powerful, and changeless God are graciously given to his creation in a language it can understand. The better we understand the Bible, its author, and our human condition, the better we will understand the why and how of what God is accomplishing in this world.

Laziness

Some of us believe that we have "gotten along fine" without investing time in reading God's Word. This laziness, compounded with busyness, causes us to a shift our responsibility onto our pastor or small-group leader. These leaders become the ones we depend on to make the Word "more palatable" and easier to digest. When they fail to accomplish this, we blame them for our lack of "being fed."

Pride-filled laziness fosters the belief that reading God's Word is a waste of time. This translates to a downward spiral of biblical illiteracy and the diminished impact Christians have on their world. As Christians look, talk, act, and live like everyone else—with similar divorce rates, attitudes toward social issues, and an inability to love—the distinctiveness between Christians and their nonbelieving counterparts grows increasingly blurry.

Opposition

We also need to be mindful of Satan's ploys, doing all he can to keep Christ's followers from reading and ingesting the words of life. If we believe God's Word is ineffective, we will choose not to read it. But once we believe and experience the part God's Word has in impacting our lives, we will experience some of what will be found in the next sections. Read on.

God's Stirring

This is God's heart for us: to know him, to be known by him, and to make him known. As we align ourselves with what God reveals to us in his Word, it will be accompanied by increased joy, understanding, confidence in obedience, and love for him and others.

God presenting us with his Word is an invitation. Accepting these daily invitations to join God in furthering our understanding of him and what he deems necessary for our lives helps us to appropriately apply and validate his truths. Our growing desire to know more appears in asking questions in order to genuinely find

answers. Notes appear in the margins of our Bibles. Our conversations become more directed to what God is doing in our lives, how he continues to prove himself faithful to his Word.

Most importantly, God uses his Word to transform our lives. These are the words of life, and as we let God have his way in us, it will always be consistent with his Word. Our obedience becomes more Spirit driven and Christlike.

Reflections from the Heart

- Genre-based hermeneutics helped me appreciate each book of the Bible in its own way. Before, I viewed the Bible as a big chunk of the same old things. I now know that each book of the Bible has its own style and must be interpreted a certain way to fully understand it. Reading the Bible from a genre-based point of view makes reading the Bible more interesting. Not that it wasn't interesting before, but now, I am enjoying the Bible to its fullest capacity. *Christine C.*

- Genre-based hermeneutics is something I have never really thought about before. It appears to give the reader a better grasp on how to read the Bible correctly, and I was just speaking with a friend recently about how many Christians in the world never bother to pick up a commentary or attempt to gain background knowledge. I hope to continue to incorporate the genre-based interpretive principles as well as use commentaries in the future. The biggest thing that I have been made aware of is the need for context, which has also contributed to my reading of a larger passage for a longer period of time. I can't believe everything I have been missing! *Andrea R.*

- When I first thought of the word *genre*, what came to mind simultaneously was different types of music. As much as I have read the Bible, never had I thought about it in different

genres. Learning about the different genres of the Bible has helped me to have an overall appreciation for the entire book, not just the New Testament but the Old Testament as well. I gained insight in so many ways, especially historically. I never thought that the background history of biblical times could have such an impact upon me. *Samantha Y.*

- I had never been introduced to different ways of understanding different books of the Bible, and I found it to be really helpful that someone acknowledged how hard it is to understand the Old Testament when you are trying to read it the same way as the New Testament. *Emilie G.*

Fill in the Blank

Employing sound genre-based hermeneutics breaks the seduction of _____ and allows me to hear God's invitation to/ for _____.

Closing Thought

God reveals himself primarily and most clearly through his Word. You will find this revelation only in the words that have been preserved and given to you as a gift of grace. Open this gift and enjoy him forever.

Helpful Reads

J. Scott Duvall and J. Daniel Hays, *Grasping God's Word: A Hands-on Approach to Reading, Interpreting, and Applying the Bible* (Grand Rapids: Zondervan, 2010).

An abridged version of the above textbook is also available.

J. Scott Duvall and J. Daniel Hays, *Journey into God's Word: Your Guide to Understanding and Applying the Bible* (Grand Rapids: Zondervan, 2008).

Gordon Fee and Douglas Stuart, *How to Read the Bible for All Its Worth*

(Grand Rapids: Zondervan, 2003).

Walt Russell, *Playing with Fire* (Colorado Springs: NavPress, 2000).

Donald Whitney, *Spiritual Disciplines for the Christian Life* (Colorado Springs: NavPress, 1991), chapter 2.

Dallas Willard, *The Spirit of the Disciplines: Understanding How God Changes Lives* (San Francisco: HarperSanFrancisco, 1991), 176–177.

2
THE WORD
GETTING INTO US

Definition: The process of absorbing the Word of God, allowing the meaning, sense, and truth of God's words to enter into the deepest recesses of our souls. Attesting to the power and commitment of God to conform us to the image of his Son, the encounter is life transforming.

Letting the Word Speak

Old Testament

Joshua 1:8: "This Book of the Law shall not depart from your mouth, but you shall meditate on it day and night, so that you may be careful to do according to all that is written in it. For then you will make your way prosperous, and then you will have good success."

The Hebrew word (*hagah*) used here for meditation involves uttering, a murmuring or whispering as in talking to yourself. Evidence of having meditated on God's law appears in Joshua's speech and actions, as he understood who God is and what he does. Obedience is the expected outcome of biblical meditation. What makes a leader and his or her leadership godly will depend in large part on how deeply God's Word has penetrated the heart.

Job 15:4: "But you are doing away with the fear of God and hindering meditation before God."

Job's three friends tried fruitlessly to identify the sin in Job's life that had led to the consequence of Job's suffering. In this second of three rounds of debate, Eliphaz resorted to accusing Job of being careless with regard to repentance and humility; therefore, God had not heard Job's meditation. Eliphaz did not understand that God hears everything, perhaps especially our meditations.

Job 23:12: "I have not departed from the commandment of his lips; I have treasured the words of his mouth more than my portion of food."

Eliphaz's third attempt to find the underlying sin that had wreaked havoc on Job was met with this fact: Job, a righteous man, cherished God's words more than the meeting of his physical needs. The words of God sustain us beyond the physical dimension; they sustain our hearts.

Psalm 1:1–3: "Blessed is the man who walks not in the counsel of the wicked, nor stands in the way of sinners, nor sits in the seat of scoffers; but his delight is in the law of the LORD, and on his law he meditates day and night. He is like a tree planted by streams of water that yields its fruit in its season, and its leaf does not wither. In all that he does, he prospers."

This is a wisdom psalm. How appropriate it is that this first psalm in the collection of 150 directs the reader in how to do life well, that is, meditate on the Word of God. As the tree planted by streams of water is constantly nourished, so the wise man or woman of God is nourished by drawing on his Word.

Psalm 19:14: "Let the words of my mouth and the meditation of my heart be acceptable in your sight, O LORD, my rock and my redeemer."

The psalmist concluded by addressing God as his refuge and champion. He desired that his inward meditations and outward

speech be aligned with God's will in acts of submission, sacrifice, and worship.

Psalm 27:4: "One thing have I asked of the LORD, that will I seek after: that I may dwell in the house of the LORD all the days of my life, to gaze upon the beauty of the LORD and to inquire in his temple."

David authored about half of the psalms, and this is one of them. The word *inquire* could also be translated *meditate*. To come before God in worship, beholding his beauty and letting it penetrate the core of our being, is a worthy ambition for those who love him.

Psalm 63:5–7: "My soul will be satisfied as with fat and rich food, and my mouth will praise you with joyful lips, when I remember you upon my bed, and meditate on you in the watches of the night; for you have been my help, and in the shadow of your wings I will sing for joy."

Sleeplessness finds its antidote: meditating on God's faithful presence, provision, and praiseworthiness. When the world gives cause to worry, God gives cause to worship.

Psalm 77:12: "I will ponder all your work, and meditate on your mighty deeds."

The author used the words *remember* and *meditate* in this community lament psalm. The people were to remember and meditate on God as the Promise Giver, the way things used to be—the good and the bad—and how God's never-changing character gives them confidence for their future.

Psalm 119. Of the twenty-one times the word *meditate* appears in the Old Testament, eight are found in this psalm alone (verses 15, 23, 27, 48, 78, 97, 99, 148). This psalm celebrates the gift of God's law as the divine guide for life, and, like Psalm 1, is a wisdom psalm. The writer credited meditation on God's Word for providing wisdom, insight, and unmatched understanding and

for enabling him to obey God. The correlation between doing life well and meditating on God's words is strong.

New Testament

Matthew 4:1–11:

> Then Jesus was led up by the Spirit into the wilderness to be tempted by the devil. And after fasting forty days and forty nights, he was hungry. And the tempter came and said to him, "If you are the Son of God, command these stones to become loaves of bread." But he answered, "It is written,
>
> > "'Man shall not live by bread alone,
> > but by every word that comes from the mouth of God.'"
>
> Then the devil took him to the holy city and set him on the pinnacle of the temple and said to him, "If you are the Son of God, throw yourself down, for it is written,
>
> > "'He will command his angels concerning you,'
> > and
> > "'On their hands they will bear you up,
> > lest you strike your foot against a stone.'"
>
> Jesus said to him, "Again it is written, 'You shall not put the Lord your God to the test.'" Again, the devil took him to a very high mountain and showed him all the kingdoms of the world and their glory. And he said to him, "All these I will give you, if you will fall down and worship me." Then Jesus said to him, "Be gone, Satan! For it is written,
>
> > "'You shall worship the Lord your God
> > and him only shall you serve.'"
>
> Then the devil left him, and behold, angels came and were ministering to him.

Of the three synoptic Gospel accounts of Jesus' temptation in the wilderness, Matthew's reveals the nature and content of Jesus' meditation most clearly. The Holy Spirit led Jesus to a wasteland, which Jews understood was inhabited by demons. His meditation on larger portions of Scripture, in this case Deuteronomy, enabled him to discern and rebuff Satan's misuse of Scripture and his attempt to derail the Messiah's commitment to seek his Father's will.

Colossians 3:1–2: "If then you have been raised with Christ, seek the things that are above, where Christ is, seated at the right hand of God. Set your minds on things that are above, not on things that are on earth."

The way we think is intimately related to the way we live. To "set your mind" calls to direct the mind toward "things above." Careful study of the Scriptures encourages meditation on God, his law, his works, and things that are heavenly and uplifting to the soul.

Food for Thought

Everybody meditates on something. If you've ever worried about anything, you've meditated, although perhaps not very productively. Biblical meditation, however, is a productive way to think, ponder, and absorb the truth of Scripture. It is the thoughtful and repetitive reflecting on the Lord and his revelation of himself in his Word.

The word *meditation* and its various forms are found primarily in the Old Testament. These Hebrew words refer to sighing, moaning, murmuring, and whispering. To meditate, then, is to speak with yourself. There's something about the inflections and emphases in the spoken sounds of the human voice that promote insight. Thought-filled talking or muttering of Scripture allows its truth to enter our innermost being where it is stored and then expressed in our behavior.

The ancient art of *lectio divina* (Latin for divine, spiritual, or sacred reading, pronounced lex.ee.oh di.vee.nuh) is a slow, meditative, contemplative reading and praying of the Scriptures. Benedict was an Italian monk who lived in the fifth and sixth centuries. His Rule for monks outlined what life in a monastery should be like. Several hours of each day were to be dedicated to the practice of *lectio divina*—a monk would read the biblical text aloud and ponder what he was hearing. Guido II, a twelfth-century French Carthusian monk, spoke of *lectio* as a process and not just a step. He is credited with having made it the four-step exercise commonly practiced today.

The placement of this chapter after one on the study of Scripture, "Getting into the Word," is intentional and strategic. For *lectio divina* to be most effective requires examining and analyzing the scriptural text. Insights from good biblical commentaries can broaden and deepen our understanding. So when the meditative processes of *lectio divina* are employed, the accurate truth found in the meaning of the biblical text finds its way into the heart.

The steps of *lectio divina* are developed here and find an interesting parallel to the natural way humans breathe.

1. **Lectio.** Related to words such as *lectern* and *lectionary*, this involves the reading and rereading of the text aloud. Like inhaling a normal breath of air, there is an openness to the word and it has a specific destination. Our breath begins to fill the lungs; God's Word begins to fill the heart.

2. **Meditatio.** Associated with *meditation* and *meditate*, this means being attentive to that word or phrase God is drawing to our focus in connecting the original meaning of that phrase with a possible correlation in life. *Meditatio* is like the respiratory pause between inhaling and exhaling when the greatest amount of oxygen moves into our bodies. Meditation makes a stronger connection between God's Word and particular life experiences or situations.

3. ***Oratio.*** In line with *orator* or *oratory*, especially as it relates to prayer, this step responds to the connections between the truth of God's Word and how it resonates with our souls. Praying God's Word is offered to him in confession, dependence, thanksgiving, understanding, forgiveness, or needy guidance. It is the prayerful encounter between our hearts and the heart of God by way of his words. As spoken words are formed in the exhale of a breath, so prayer is the expression of the reality of our intimate relationship with God.

4. ***Contemplatio.*** From the same word family as *contemplation*, this last step is the sustained communion with God. Though some exchange occurs throughout the breath cycle, the respiratory pause just after an exhaled breath pictures the beginning of the settling of that oxygen into our bodies that continues to enable healthy cells to function with optimal performance. Our sensitivity to God's Spirit is heightened as we surrender to the infusing truth of God's Word and discover our responsibility in living out what is now settled in our hearts, for from our hearts flow the issues of life (Proverbs 4:23).

True knowledge of the Word requires meditation on the Word; true meditation on the Word requires knowledge of the Word.

How To

We do not need to be experts in the art of *lectio* to glean its benefits. An environment conducive to the study of and meditation on God's Word is one that permits silence and is favorable to reflection and prayer. The time afforded for *lectio* should be when we are rousing from adequate sleep and/or when the prime part of our day can be dedicated to settling into the presence of God. Though this may vary with different life stages, its effectiveness need not be diminished.

Pitfalls

Skepticism

Some may be a little uncomfortable with the fact that *lectio divina* has monastic roots. Perhaps we fear the slippery slope of Catholic leanings. But the real question to ask is, "Is it biblical?" Do the elements appear in the pages of Scripture, or are they exampled in the life of Jesus? Eugene Peterson summarized the components of *lectio divina* with "Read. Think. Pray. Live"—each soundly echoed in the pages of God's Word.[1]

Selectivity

Another pitfall can be seen in a question a colleague posed: "Do you find that all people want to do is *lectio* without the investment of applying sound interpretive principles to determine the meaning of a passage?" *Lectio divina* that ignores the critical step of study and knowledge of God's Word compromises the process of getting his Word into us by its failure to ensure the heart is receiving the true meaning and intent of the Scriptures.

God's Stirring

When God's Word settles more deeply into our souls, we are placed in a better position for his Holy Spirit to work in and through us. This increased sensitivity to God's movements is evidenced by a greater ability to respond in obedience. As we become more attuned to his promptings, our obedient response to those promptings becomes more probable. As God continues to prove himself worthy of our obedience, our trust in what he is doing and wants to do is strengthened. Our words and silences are expressed with greater wisdom and our accompanying actions reflect him more accurately.

Reflections from the Heart

- *Lectio Divina* complemented by genre-based hermeneutics is the perfect couple in one's spiritual formation. When I incorporated *lectio divina* and did not use genre-based hermeneutics, I did not learn all that the author intended for me to discover. I am glad that I learned the process of studying Scripture through genre-based hermeneutics. Before this class, I went to my Bible and did not know where to begin. I knew to not just read a psalm a day, but I wanted to know more than that. I wanted to learn how to *really* study the Bible. But, whenever I opened my Bible, I did not know exactly what to do. Genre-based hermeneutics as well as *lectio divina* has helped me to begin this process of actually *studying* God's Word. I will continue to use this method of studying Scripture, because it not only helped with my understanding of the Bible, but also helped me to get in a daily rhythm of meaningfully studying God's Word. *Natalie R.*

- I had been previously familiar with principles from *lectio*; however, I had never been exposed to *lectio* itself. After I learned the principles of this, it very much helped my hermeneutics and interpretation of Scripture. It caused the Word of God to go deeper into my heart and caused me to think about the Word more often and in a more contemplative way. *Austin B.*

- Merely using commentaries and looking at history and other interpretive help texts is just not enough to further one's own relationship with God. Because we were urged to meditate, contemplate, pray, and live on these passages, my heart has experienced growth and trust in the Lord. I am so appreciative of *lectio divina* and how we were able to incorporate it, . . . because it made me more aware of the Lord's constant presence in my life and how I can glorify him through every one of my actions. *Bethany C.*

- The process of *lectio divina* is wonderfully beneficial to spiritual formation and an important aid to Scripture reading. It is easy to be impatient when reading the Bible and cruise through

large portions without giving it much thought or time to sink into the soul. I myself often have this problem. It is sometimes as if God has nagged me enough to make me give up the fight and get out my Bible, but then I read like a stubborn child doing his chores poorly. I would read through a passage just to reach the ending point that I already set for myself. As the years have gone by, I have become better than this, but not by much, and the whole time I have been robbing myself of soul-filling nourishment. Forgive my many analogies, but what *lectio divina* does is not only slow me down to fully enjoy and be blessed by the spiritual food of God's Word, but it turns this food gourmet. *Lectio divina* is a process of preparing the mind and soul and making God's Word powerful and meaningful, as is its purpose, to impact the soul. *Jeffrey S.*

Fill in the Blank

Meditating on God's Word breaks the seduction of _____ and allows me to hear God's invitation to/for _____.

Closing Thought

Meditating on God's Word is like a soaking rain that reaches the root of the tree, strengthens its branches, and enables it to bear fruit. It is God's gracious way of making his divine imprint on our hearts.

Helpful Reads

Richard Foster, *Life with God: Reading the Bible for Spiritual Transformation* (New York: HarperOne, 2008).

Henry Holloman, *The Forgotten Blessing* (Nashville: Word Publishing, 1999), chapter 10.

Mario Masini, *Lectio Divina: An Ancient Prayer That Is Ever New* (New

York: Alba House, 1998).

John Ortberg, *The Life You've Always Wanted: Spiritual Disciplines for Ordinary People* (Grand Rapids: Zondervan, 2002), chapter 11.

Richard Peace, *Contemplative Bible Reading: Experiencing God through Scripture* (Colorado Springs: NavPress, 1998).

Donald Whitney, *Spiritual Disciplines for the Christian Life* (Colorado Springs: NavPress, 1991), chapter 3.

Knowing Grace

3
SILENCE AND SOLITUDE:
THE SOUNDTRACK OF INTIMACY

Definition: The stillness of time and place where you are alert to the rumblings of the soul and the impressions of God and where you find a deep willingness to stay and return.

Letting the Word Speak

Old Testament

1 Kings 19:11–12: "And he said, 'Go out and stand on the mount before the LORD.' And behold, the LORD passed by, and a great and strong wind tore the mountains and broke in pieces the rocks before the LORD, but the LORD was not in the wind. And after the wind an earthquake, but the LORD was not in the earthquake. And after the earthquake a fire, but the LORD was not in the fire. And after the fire the sound of a low whisper."

Elijah stood on Mount Horeb (also known as Mount Sinai, where Moses saw God and was given the Ten Commandments), dispirited by the unrelenting personal attack of Queen Jezebel, whose name means "Where is the prince [Baal]?" She pitted herself against Elijah, whose name means "Yahweh is my God." He is found frightened, despondent, and hiding in a cave when God directs him to stand outside on the mountain to give him a gift

of his presence. In usual fashion God's great dramatic power is demonstrated in the wind, earthquake, and fire; but God is not in any of those. God's confirmation of the frail Elijah was found in the "thin silence" of a powerful God.

Lamentations 3:28: "Let him sit alone in silence when it is laid on him."

Lamentations 3:22–23 provides the words to a much-beloved hymn, "Great Is Thy Faithfulness," and precede Jeremiah's own lament as he was personally experiencing God's judgment of disaster on Jerusalem and the people of God for their disobedience and unfaithfulness. Yet in this terrible suffering and misery, he wrote of the things he knew to be true of God—that he is a God of love and compassion. Jeremiah knew that it is good to seek this God, at all costs, with watchful expectancy and glad submission.

 Habakkuk 2:20: "But the Lord is in his holy temple; let all the earth keep silence before him."

This prophet questioned God. How could God remain silent and apparently inactive when the ferociously evil, cruel, inhumane, idol-worshiping Babylonians were encroaching on Judah? Would God use a massively evil nation to discipline a less evil one: Judah? The idols of both nations were lifeless, powerless, and silent; yet the silence commanded by Habakkuk was the awe-filled, worshipful response to the presence of God himself.

New Testament

Matthew 11:28–30: "Come to me, all who labor and are heavy laden, and I will give you rest. Take my yoke upon you, and learn from me, for I am gentle and lowly in heart, and you will find rest for your souls. For my yoke is easy, and my burden is light."

Here is Jesus' invitation. It is in stark contrast to the burdensome weight placed on souls by society and culture. Worn-out souls need the kind of divine replenishment and rest that only

Jesus offers. His Spirit strengthens the sons and daughters of God as they walk one foot in front of the other in the right direction.

Mark 1:35: "And rising very early in the morning, while it was still dark, he departed and went out to a desolate place, and there he prayed."

Jesus' popularity was on the rise. Notice how early he had to get up and out in order to avoid the crowds. Jesus talked to his Father where and when he would not be interrupted, because the disciples would come searching for him.

Mark 6:31–32: "And he said to them, 'Come away by yourselves to a desolate place and rest a while.' For many were coming and going, and they had no leisure even to eat. And they went away in the boat to a desolate place by themselves."

The disciples were so steeped in the adrenaline rush from the swarming crowds that encircled Jesus; they had not even taken the time to eat. Jesus knew the healthy importance of his disciples going away to be alone with him, so he bid his exhausted friends to come to a place to rest. Notice the relationship between Jesus' presence and rest.

Mark 6:45–46: "Immediately he made his disciples get into the boat and go before him to the other side, to Bethsaida, while he dismissed the crowd. And after he had taken leave of them, he went up on the mountain to pray."

The people in the crowd of more than five thousand, each one miraculously fed from the multiplied fish and barley loaves, were not the only ones to leave this desolate place with deep impressions of Jesus the Messiah. Imagine the thoughts running through the disciples' minds as they pushed off from the shore and headed toward another part of the lake.

There was a lot on Jesus' mind and heart, too. Antagonism and hostility toward him was mounting. His praying connected him with God. It was about 3 a.m., and from his spot on the mountain, Jesus could see his disciples on the lake as the winds began to stir up the waters. Soon the disciples would see a glimpse of Jesus for who he is, as the Messiah walked on water.

Luke 5:16: "But he would withdraw to desolate places and pray."

Luke recorded Jesus' praying a number of times. This rhythm even shows up in the way Luke used the Greek language in this verse to reveal that it was a regular practice of Jesus to withdraw and pray. Jesus didn't allow the growing crowds or increasing fame to control his schedule; he let God do that.

Food for Thought

The speed at which we choose to live may force us to fit more tasks into our days. To try to simplify her life, a friend of mine used to dress her children the night before for early morning swim lessons. They slept in their swimwear instead of their pajamas. For her morning cup of coffee, she bought a programmable coffeemaker. Because she preferred her coffee with cream and sugar, she placed perfectly measured amounts of these into the coffeemaker's basket. Brewed coffee would become perfectly blended as it found its way into the waiting pot. The perfect cup of coffee was in hand as she stood at the open front door, watching her bathing-suit-clad children march sleepily toward the car.

It seems that the more time we have, the greater the tendency to fill it with more things to do. Instead of relishing the relaxing moments afforded by time-saving devices, we have chosen to use the additional hours to accomplish more. Ironically, we find ourselves busier than ever and at an increasing speed.

Here are some observed symptoms of what speed looks like when it gets the best of us. We want things to run faster: computers, cars, appointments, meals, meetings, decision making, and checkout lines. Speed has found its way into the very heart of how we want to live.

The second observation is that we tend to have superficial relationships. Our calendars dictate whether or not relationships are feasible. This relationship-by-appointment places a higher value on convenience than on human need. We invest less in meaningful dialogue; conversations become shallow and phony. Our relationships have become the same.

The last observation regards self-centeredness. We expect the world to revolve our needs. I once saw a personal license plate that attested to this. It read, "WA2BZ4U" (way too busy for you). This illustrates the priority placed on our own agendas at the cost of relationships. Here's a sobering question: How often have I said that to God? Our self-promoting plans become a higher priority than the people around us and God.

Jesus knew the subtle and magnetic lure of speed. He also knew it was important to get away, not for the sake of getting away, but for being with his Father. The antidote for the crash-and-burn of speed is silence and solitude. Following an exhilarating time of ministry where the disciples were casting out demons, healing the sick, and preaching, Jesus and his disciples crossed the lake for a time of silence and solitude. Instead, they were met by five thousand or more people. More ministry was being demanded. The Messiah's compassion on the crowd was clear, as he first filled them with spiritual food and then with physical food. Scripture doesn't record the disciples' disappointment. Maybe it was because of the time they *did* have with Jesus on the boat. They and Jesus seized the "boat moments." Perhaps the brief word, comforting touch, approving glance, or affirming smile from their Master assured them that he could be trusted, even in seemingly chaotic times.

At times we are given the extraordinary opportunities to spend a significant amount of time with God, listening and receiving. Removed from the rush of our days, we are allowed to develop and savor the depth of intimacy with God. These times help foster the ability to seize the "boat moments" of our more

ordinary days—snatched glimpses, prodding nudges, a needed touch, and choicest words from the Master. These sound bites of silence and solitude are not a substitute for those extended times, but they are not necessarily void of breadth and depth.

How To

Be intentional in seeking out time and space for silence and solitude, challenging yourself with the length and depth of time. A period of three to six hours is a good beginning. Choose a quiet place, perhaps in nature, devoid of manufactured noise. Present yourself before God in prayer. It may be helpful to list, one by one, the competing thoughts, challenges, and stress points of your life and then place each one in the hands of God. The purpose is not only to unclutter our minds and lives, though that is a frequently experienced result, but also to humbly engage in listening from the depths of our souls to the ever-present voice of God. The rhythm of these extended times helps train us to be attentive to and to seize the "boat moments."

You may find yourself eventually driving in a slower lane, taking a walk during a lunch break, or choosing a longer line at the checkout stand, preferring to intentionally convert those times to connecting with God. The goal isn't always the amount of time spent but the depth of communion, growing more familiar with his voice and impulses of his Spirit. It will be easier to slip into periodic times of silence and solitude throughout the day, having grown familiar with what that time in deep communion with God looks, feels, and sounds like.

Because we often hide behind our words, our silence forces us to recognize the escapes we have grown accustomed to using. Our being silent fosters the practice of stopping the tongue, so as to gain better control of it. Listen for his voice; it will always be consistent with his Word, the clearest revelation of his character. This helps in discerning whether the voice we hear is his or ours. As you progress in your communion with God, you may hear

him ask, "Will you trust me?" He will see how you live out your answer.

Sometimes it is helpful to bring your Bible to your time in silence and solitude, but, here again, be aware of even hiding behind the Bible to avoid having a two-way dialogue with God. Let him speak. Sometimes the Scriptures we have hidden in our hearts, or that we have recently studied, can be fodder for our prayers.

Pitfalls

Fear

Some of us don't want to hear God. We expect to hear condemnation and criticism. But when we accept his invitation to come and join him, he's not waiting there with a sledgehammer. He has been waiting, wanting you to hear for yourself of his love, forgiveness, and guidance for you. In his presence is peace.

Competition

The world will scream that there is no need for such a waste of time. The world demands productivity, and we comply with overbooking our days. Empty spaces in our calendars threaten our perceived worth. The awkwardness and discomfort in discovering more about the true self cause some to rush through silence and solitude.

Additionally, our minds can be flooded with wandering thoughts. With both these scenarios, instead of trying to suppress or ignore them, bring them to God. Our propensity for speed crowds out a high-held value of God's kingdom. We need to be intentional and create space to be alone with God—this is where genuine communion takes place.

God's Stirring

Normal sounds may seem louder, almost irritating; you may

resonate more with the sounds of silence. As you grow familiar with the sounds of silence, give yourself permission to stay in that moment, allowing God's Spirit to bring whatever he wants to your mind. Give his Spirit the opportunity to have a say. His voice is one of grace and loving firmness, never of condemnation or faultfinding.

A new appreciation for the potential held in your spoken words emerges. The words we speak become more meaningful and potent after meeting with God in silence and solitude. The other-centeredness created in our words also shows up in our serving others.

Reflections from the Heart

- I went in thinking that silence and solitude were just descriptors of the setting I need to get to so I can really focus on praying, reading, and reflection. What God revealed to me after about forty-five minutes of frustrating prayer is that silence and solitude were not just a place I needed to reach; rather, they were descriptors of what state my soul should be in. And from then on I chose to just listen to God. At first it was quiet, my heart was calm and at rest, and I was not sure quite what would happen. Then God showed up. He did not talk audibly, obviously, nor did he make clear my future or "what I must do," but in my heart I know he clearly addressed a lot of the things I am going through and wrestling with and made it explicitly clear, even to my racing heart, that he deeply, boldly loves me. *Blake H.*

- I was reluctant to do silence and solitude. First of all, I was coming into it with an unforgiving heart. I had just gotten into a fight with my mom and wasn't ready to forgive or reconcile just yet. I thought God would convict me and I would have to do something about it. It was burdening me. Secondly, I doubted he would just show up on my time, I thought an

hour isn't enough, and I had a list of things I needed to get done before the baby wakes up. Anyhow, I read the chapter on silence and solitude, and my attitude changed from dreading the time to a time I was really looking forward to and desperately needed. I started my silence and solitude by pouring out all that was on my heart, giving him all my worries and thoughts, even the ones I mentioned above. I was essentially giving him all my burdens, and then I realized the weight was starting to come off my shoulders. This thought entered my mind: believe God's presence is always with me. . . . and then, I just sat still, quiet . . . realizing that the Almighty was with me . . . Another thought came to mind: he's always willing to seize those boat moments with me. I am worthy enough that he wants to spend time with me. At that moment, I was focused on God and on God only. The silence and solitude helped me to realize I needed to put my focus back on my Father, not on my issues. Another thought came to mind: focus on how God is loving me; look for it daily. I was reluctant because I thought God had certain expectations from me, but what he wanted to do was take those from me, stay mindful of his presence, and look for his expressions of love for me . . . completely different from what I thought he wanted. It helped me prioritize what was most important, the vertical relationship before the horizontal. *Cathy L.*

- During my time in solitude, I heard more than I have heard in a long time. . . . Once you have refrained from using words at all, you see afterward that every word you do use has massive weight to it. You are keen not to want to use them in a frivolous or unnecessary manner. It showed me how much I normally rely on words to justify and build myself up. I am someone who truly wants to be liked. When I am not talking, I do not have the power to show how "cool" I am. So when I was not talking, I felt like I was allowing God to be in control

rather than using words to try to control how others saw me. *Ben M.*

- Eating by myself in silence made me feel really alone. After I finished eating, God hit me with my conscience. I was walking past the milk dispensers when I saw a kid who is always alone and doesn't seem to have many friends. I didn't say anything to him as I passed him, easily letting him walk by because I was trying to have a day of silence. Then God quietly spoke to me about that: "You let it slide to say hi quickly to your friends on your day of silence with me, but when you pass someone who really could use a smile and a friend, you ignore him? Which is more like me?" *Matt H.*

- Unfortunately I wasn't focused on him and waiting and talking to him all three hours I was there, but the times that I wasn't distracted by the air conditioning, hearing people come in and out, and also sleeping, were very good. One thing that I have to talk about is what God showed me about my mom. I was sitting there, praying for my family, and once I came across my mom, I just started crying. I hadn't called her in a long time, and I didn't want to call her. Some things had been going on, and I just didn't want to face them. God showed me my bitterness and how I needed to talk to her. I cried and cried for the longest time. Then I just sat and listened in silence. I knew that God had been working in my heart, and it wasn't until this silence and solitude that I was broken by him. I had been praying about the situation, and I also had fasted not too long before as well. But I didn't just sit and wait for him to speak to me. I had been too busy trying to figure out what to do. God was waiting for me to be quiet so that he could work in me. *Moriah J.*

Fill in the Blank

Silence and solitude break the seduction of _____ and allow me to hear God's invitation to/for _____.

Closing Thought

Speed takes us nowhere fast. Instead, recognize the sweetness of being invited to be still and quiet before God. In being more attentively present with God, you can become more attentively present with others and with yourself.

Helpful Reads

Richard Foster, *Celebration of Discipline: The Path to Spiritual Growth* (San Francisco: HarperSanFrancisco, 1998), chapter 7.

John Ortberg, *The Life You've Always Wanted: Spiritual Disciplines for Ordinary People* (Grand Rapids: Zondervan, 2002), chapter 5.

Donald Whitney, *Spiritual Disciplines for the Christian Life* (Colorado Springs: NavPress, 1991), chapter 10.

Dallas Willard, *The Spirit of the Disciplines: Understanding How God Changes Lives* (San Francisco: HarperSanFrancisco, 1991), 160–165.

4
FASTING:
FAST FOOD

Definition: The response to God's prompting to intentionally deny the ever self-pleasing *me* for a period of time from something (1) I know I need, (2) I have been convinced I need, or (3) I have been convinced I am entitled to have. We should fast for a period long enough to come to the point of recognizing the adhesive grasp something has over us and hearing our response to God's question, "Am I enough for you?"

Letting the Word Speak

Old Testament

1 Samuel 7:6: "So they gathered at Mizpah and drew water and poured it out before the LORD and fasted on that day and said there, 'We have sinned against the LORD.' And Samuel judged the people of Israel at Mizpah."

Samuel led this public ceremony in Mizpah, in which Israel confessed national sin. Both the fasting and the pouring of water (the washing away of corporate guilt) expressed sorrow and repentance. An attitude of repentance is a sign of a readied heart.

2 Samuel 12:15-17: "Then Nathan went to his house. And the LORD afflicted the child that Uriah's wife bore to David, and he

became sick. David therefore sought God on behalf of the child. And David fasted and went in and lay all night on the ground. And the elders of his house stood beside him, to raise him from the ground, but he would not, nor did he eat food with them."

Israel's most beloved king petitioned God in fasting. When his infant son became ill, David still hoped that the Lord might change his mind and let the child live. In his fast, David aligned himself with God and accepted his decision.

Nehemiah 1:4: "As soon as I heard these words I sat down and wept and mourned for days, and I continued fasting and praying before the God of heaven."

Upon receiving word of Jerusalem's devastation with walls broken and gates destroyed, Nehemiah responded in tearful concern and fasting that strengthened his intercession before God. Nehemiah knew God's Word and understood who God is. He was able to trust the God who is sufficient and who demonstrates his steadfast love to those who keep his commandments.

Esther 4:16: "Go, gather all the Jews to be found in Susa, and hold a fast on my behalf, and do not eat or drink for three days, night or day. I and my young women will also fast as you do. Then I will go to the king, though it is against the law, and if I perish, I perish."

Esther's request for fasting—implying prayer as well—revealed her dependence on others for support and her need for God's intervention. Fasting was usually practiced during the day, so a three-day continuous fast shows the urgency of this matter. Indeed, Esther had a life-threatening decision before her, and the fast enabled her to focus on her relationship with God. She would resolve to place her life in God's providential care.

Isaiah 58:3–7:

"Why have we fasted, and you see it not?
Why have we humbled ourselves, and you take no knowledge of it?"

Behold, in the day of your fast you seek your own
pleasure,
 and oppress all your workers.
Behold, you fast only to quarrel and to fight
 and to hit with a wicked fist.
Fasting like yours this day
 will not make your voice to be heard on high.
Is such the fast that I choose,
 a day for a person to humble himself?
Is it to bow down his head like a reed,
 and to spread sackcloth and ashes under him?
Will you call this a fast,
 and a day acceptable to the LORD?
Is not this the fast that I choose:
 to loose the bonds of wickedness,
 to undo the straps of the yoke,
to let the oppressed go free,
 and to break every yoke?
Is it not to share your bread with the hungry
 and bring the homeless poor into your house;
when you see the naked, to cover him,
 and not to hide yourself from your own flesh?

The Israelites' impressive piety was only a ploy for manipulating God, and they were offended that their religiosity didn't work. They invested in false confidence. Here, the wrong reason to fast is revealed: to twist the arm of God. Just a couple of verses later, God gave the heart model for fasting: do away with blame shifting, and give of yourself on behalf of the poor and oppressed. Evidence of true piety is treating others with respect, justice, and kindness, a theme characteristic of the writings of the Old Testament prophets.

Jeremiah 14:11–12: "The LORD said to me: 'Do not pray for the welfare of this people. Though they fast, I will not hear

their cry, and though they offer burnt offering and grain offering, I will not accept them. But I will consume them by the sword, by famine, and by pestilence.'"

Fasting without the right heart motivation is just another weight-loss program. Here is a rare instance when God said he would not accept these intercessions because of the hollowness of the intent. God doesn't play games. He desires us to be genuine because he is always genuine. Empty religiosity, just going through the motions, never has impressed God and never will.

New Testament

Matthew 4:2: "And after fasting forty days and forty nights, he was hungry."

Forty days is about the longest a human can fast before incurring permanent physical harm. Jesus' forty-day fast brought intense communion with God that readied him for Satan's attempt to foil the divine plan to redeem humanity by disqualifying the Messiah. Jesus' victory over Satan and perfect obedience to the Father prepared Jesus for his earthly ministry.

Matthew 6:16–18: "And when you fast, do not look gloomy like the hypocrites, for they disfigure their faces that their fasting may be seen by others. Truly, I say to you, they have received their reward. But when you fast, anoint your head and wash your face, that your fasting may not be seen by others but by your Father who is in secret. And your Father who sees in secret will reward you."

Jesus assumed his disciples would fast because he said, "*When* you fast . . ." It is easy to think that fasting can make someone holier or that fasting is a sure way of earning spiritual brownie points with God. Publicizing your fasting with words or with prideful looks or with body language is a way to flaunt false devotion. Fasting is a matter of hearts: yours and God's.

Matthew 9:14–15: "Then the disciples of John came to

him, saying, 'Why do we and the Pharisees fast, but your disciples do not fast?' And Jesus said to them, 'Can the wedding guests mourn as long as the bridegroom is with them? The days will come when the bridegroom is taken away from them, and then they will fast.'" (Also see Mark 2:18–19 and Luke 5:33–35.)

More than transcending the legalistic-prone rituals of Pharisaical religiosity, the practice of fasting was expected of Christ's followers as they humbly sought the presence of God and spiritual growth.

Acts 13:1–3: "Now there were in the church at Antioch prophets and teachers, Barnabas, Simeon who was called Niger, Lucius of Cyrene, Manaen a member of the court of Herod the tetrarch, and Saul. While they were worshiping the Lord and fasting, the Holy Spirit said, 'Set apart for me Barnabas and Saul for the work to which I have called them.' Then after fasting and praying they laid their hands on them and sent them off."

Under the guidance of the Holy Spirit, the church was readied for its greatest step: taking the message of the gospel out to the world. Its magnitude required the guidance of the Holy Spirit. Men of varying backgrounds and ethnicities were united in this task to fast—and worship and pray—deepening their sensitivity to the communication and direction of God's Spirit.

Food for Thought

Tyler was a confident twenty-year-old when he announced his "plans" for a road trip. The conversation went something like this:

Tyler: Mom, I'm going on a road trip.

Me: Oh. Where?

Tyler: Oh, I don't know. Maybe I'll just drive to northern California.

Me: Anywhere specific?

Tyler: No.

Me: Do you know where you might make some stops?
Tyler: No.
Me: How long will you go for?
Tyler: I don't know.
Me: Will you be driving with anyone?
Tyler: No, just me.
Me: When do you want to go?
Tyler: In a couple weeks.

You can imagine the questions and doubts I had about this whole idea, but you might also understand that an outright "That's one of the dumbest things I've ever heard! Of course you cannot go on such a trip!" would not work. I was prompted to remain silent.

That week I was exercising a fast from any media sounds on my commute to campus. During this thirty-minute drive, I seized the time to draw close to God by listening to him and praying (with eyes open of course!). While meeting with God, I noticed something. Twice I watched my hand reach for the radio. As I began to notice this seemingly automatic motion, I asked God to show me in that moment what was triggering my distraction. It seems that my thoughts of Tyler's upcoming trip brought a sense of anxiety, and my reflex was to extend my arm toward the radio's power button. I had sought to pacify my immediate worry with music, forsaking the opportunity to bring the matter more fully before God. How often have I chosen a recorded melody over the caring voice of the One who actually wants my burdens? God made us dependent beings. If we're not dependent on him, we will be dependent on something or someone else. Oh, but how God delights in my realizing and fully expressing my absolute dependence on him (Psalm 147:11; Matthew 5:4; 1 Peter 5:7).

By the way, Tyler didn't go on the road trip as he had "planned."

How To

Start off with a prayer for humility because it is humbling to realize how distracted and distant from God we have become. In seeking God, we quickly learn more about ourselves and what has control over us. A one-day fast is the normal fasting period. Starting after lunch on one day and ending at the beginning of lunch the following day is an easy way to begin. Remember to drink plenty of water. Having fruit juices or other liquid nourishment (e.g., Ensure) available can help your first fasting attempts. Add to this a media fast, refraining from any use of computers, the Internet, Facebook, MySpace, cell phones, iPod, television, radio, movies, and so on. As you experience the "hunger" or "withdrawal" from these things, as you see or feel the pull of self, intentionally direct your thoughts to God. If you have a preexisting medical condition that might be compromised by this exercise, ask your doctor for the acceptable guidelines for this day of fasting.

Pitfalls

Fear

The thought of fasting can be anxiety raising, especially when we've grown so accustomed to immediate and sustained gratification. In our culture it sounds absurd to deprive ourselves of anything. Nurturing a growing dependence on God is countercultural to our contemporary world, which is driven by the created need and dependence on having more—be it food, control, money, or things.

Fasting is the mirror that reveals the dependencies, addictions, and worldly attachments that have become part of us. There can be much trepidation in assessing our true spiritual status quo through fasting, especially now that we have a new generation of social-networking addicts.

Allow God to know your fears, and let him again prove his graciousness. Verbally acknowledge to the Lord your fears, which

he already knows. Biblical fasting will take humility to exercise, but it is good soil where Christlike humility can grow. Interestingly, the word for fasting in Leviticus 16:29 is rendered, "Humble your souls" (NASB).

Substitutions

Though the world uses fasting as a form of dieting, protesting, or connecting with the self, biblical fasting differs in purpose and outcome. Observe how the self bulldozes its way to the front of the line. It manipulates and rationalizes—or more accurately, "rational lies"—to meet its wants. Be alert to the ways the self will seek substitutes to engage in as attempts are made to direct its attention toward the Lord. The propensity to seek self-entitlements may be very strong, but these can be thwarted by fasting.

God's Stirring

Hunger pangs will come. So will media urges. You will reach for your cell phone, computer, or the power button for your car's sound system. In those very acts the self struggles for the reign it has been accustomed to exercising. You will have front-row seats as pride comes to its defense. Ask God to alert you to what is on your mind when tempted to reach for the very thing that seeks to divert your attention away from him. By his grace, with each victory, you will grow more alert to his nudges and voice, his comfort and peace, his guidance and power.

This growing awareness of the invisible divine world intersecting our temporal, material world is evidenced by thankfulness, humility, and confession. "Coincidences" are unmasked as ordained events laced with his provision and presence. Our dependence quotient expands as God consistently proves himself worthy of our trust.

Reflections from the Heart

- Within the first few hours of being completely free from

media, I began to feel disconnected, incomplete, and out of touch. I felt like I was ignored and abandoned. Something . . . dug up old feelings of hurt and being abandoned by my parents. I didn't like this feeling at all. I watched people to see if there was anyone I knew that I could connect with. I continued to reach for my phone that wasn't there. I asked God why I would continually reach for my phone and what emotion led me to continue to do that. He revealed to me that it was out of fear. Fear of being stuck alone like I have been for so many years before. I am so dependent on people that there is no room for God to meet my needs. *Zachary G.*

- I was faced with the stark realization of how much I am controlled by media like movies and TV. If I am having a bad day, or need a mental break, I am more apt to calm myself and vacate reality for a while by escaping into the fiction of a TV show rather than calling on Jesus, asking him to give me peace, and spending time seeking his healing in prayer. What a false sense of renewal I have been seeking after! *Tiffany M.*

- During this week of my fast, I became conscious to a sudden urge to go on Facebook. I asked the Lord to reveal the belief or thought behind this urge to check my Facebook. I realized that I was getting caught up with the approval of my friends' comments toward me on my "wall" and was feeding in to it as my identity. I did not like what I realized. *Reggie C.*

- Me fast, no way; that's not for me; I need to eat. As I read more of the chapter, I was convicted and encouraged to seek HIM by doing the very thing I really didn't want to do. So I decided to go with it. The next thirty-six hours of my life will forever change me. I experienced God in a way I thought I had . . . but nothing compares to fasting, to get strength, not of myself but from God . . . taking away the very thing I THOUGHT I needed, and realizing I needed

something (someone) else more. I quickly came face to face with the thing I didn't want to admit . . . that I want to be in CONTROL. This control has taken on many different shapes, but nonetheless CONTROL is what I wanted. God took me to different passages in the Bible to gently remind me who really IS in control of everything. But, in this process, he also pointed me to different passages that dealt with different areas of my life that have just left me speechless. . . . I have shed tears of joy and appreciation because God really knows my heart, even when I don't. I still have a lot to process from this experience, and I still have a lot of work to be done in me, but I want God to be in CONTROL, not me. May his perfect work be done! I have learned a lot from this experience, and that is, when God reveals the sin in my life, he does it with LOVE, GRACE, and MERCY. BTW . . . this was my first time fasting, and it was definitely an experience I will NEVER forget! I have experienced God so intimately. . . . I have been left with a desire to experience him again the same way. *Elizabeth H.*

- I began my fast on Friday morning and before the morning was even up, I discovered that I was reaching for my iPod at various times during the day, but because I didn't have it, I was unable to fill my ears with music. I was curious and began to pray to God, asking if he'd show me why I kept reaching for it. After about the third or fourth time, it hit me: I reached for my iPod when I needed to feel good, when I needed to forget a hurt or a thought. I had conditioned music in my life to be a comfort for me, something I could go to and not feel judged or belittled or hurt. The problem being I would forgo speaking with my Father about my feelings. . . . I learned that I use technology as my hideout and music as my safe place. *Cory M.*

Fill in the Blank

Fasting breaks the seduction of _____ and allows me to hear God's invitation to/for _____.

Closing Thought

The full benefit of the soul-nourishing times of coming into God's presence is maximized when we can exercise control over the temporary, unfulfilling fixes of downloaded tunes, poked walls, or a demanding appetite. God's gracious way of showing you more about you is his invitation to know he is all you really need.

Helpful Reads

Lynne M. Baab, *Fasting: Spiritual Freedom beyond Our Appetites* (Downers Grove: InterVarsity Press, 2006).

Richard Foster, *Celebration of Discipline: The Path to Spiritual Growth* (San Francisco: HarperSanFrancisco, 1998), chapter 4.

Klaus Issler, *Wasting Time with God: A Christian Spirituality of Friendship with God* (Downers Grove: InterVarsity Press, 2001), chapter 4.

Donald Whitney, *Spiritual Disciplines for the Christian Life* (Colorado Springs: NavPress, 1991), chapter 9.

Dallas Willard, *The Spirit of the Disciplines: Understanding How God Changes Lives* (San Francisco: HarperSanFrancisco, 1991), 166–168.

Knowing Grace

5
PRAYER:
THE RESPIRATION
OF THE SOUL

Definition: Personally and deeply communicating and communing with God in words, thoughts, cries, or sighs. As we listen, we open ourselves to the divine impressions he places on the soul.

Letting the Word Speak

Old Testament

Psalm 10:17: "O Lord, you hear the desire of the afflicted; you will strengthen their heart; you will incline your ear."

The oppressed and defenseless are easily wronged and exploited. God's people should extend his love, justice, and care to others. We need to stay mindful that the day of judgment may be delayed, but it is not canceled. In the meanwhile, the psalmist interceded on behalf of the oppressed, praying for strengthened courage amid affliction. He had confidence that God would have the last word.

Psalm 27:4: "One thing have I asked of the Lord, that will I seek after: that I may dwell in the house of the Lord all the days of my life, to gaze upon the beauty of the Lord and to inquire in his temple."

The temple was the visible expression of God's presence. In single-minded worship, David declared that there is nothing better than to be fully present with God. He wanted nothing to get in the way of experiencing God's presence and his gracious kindness.

Psalm 38:9: "O Lord, all my longing is before you; my sighing is not hidden from you."

Sometimes all we can offer God are the sighs of loneliness, anguish, resignation, and helplessness. He hears them all.

Psalm 91:14–16: "Because he holds fast to me in love, I will deliver him; I will protect him, because he knows my name. When he calls to me, I will answer him; I will be with him in trouble; I will rescue him and honor him. With long life I will satisfy him and show him my salvation."

God speaks in these verses, promising three things to those who trust and love him: (1) protection in danger, (2) an answer in trouble, and (3) long life and salvation. The Maker of the universe, the One who created our souls, has something to say to each of us.

Psalm 103:13–14: "As a father shows compassion to his children, so the LORD shows compassion to those who fear him. For he knows our frame; he remembers that we are dust."

God knows our frailties, faults, and finiteness. Unlike our earthly fathers, God is the perfect Father who is patient and kind and understands everything about his children. We need not fear approaching our heavenly Father.

Nehemiah 2:4: "Then the king said to me, 'What are you requesting?' So I prayed to the God of heaven."

Nehemiah felt so close to God that it was automatic for him to speak to God and the king almost simultaneously. His silently speaking to God before answering the king reveals a natural habit of prayer.

Nehemiah 9:6: "You are the LORD, you alone. You have made heaven, the heaven of heavens, with all their host, the earth and all that is on it, the seas and all that is in them; and you preserve all of them; and the host of heaven worships you."

God alone is given credit for the whole of all creation, and prayer can focus on his creative activity. Because he is sovereign over everything, we must ask according to his will. The more we understand and accept his sovereignty, the more our prayers will reflect our wanting his will.

New Testament

Matthew 6:5–8:

> And when you pray, you must not be like the hypocrites. For they love to stand and pray in the synagogues and at the street corners, that they may be seen by others. Truly, I say to you, they have received their reward. But when you pray, go into your room and shut the door and pray to your Father who is in secret. And your Father who sees in secret will reward you. And when you pray, do not heap up empty phrases as the Gentiles do, for they think that they will be heard for their many words. Do not be like them, for your Father knows what you need before you ask him.

God is not interested in the ways religious imposters seek to build their own reputations. Their reward is the flattery they receive from those who have bought into the deception. God is more concerned with motivation. When we convert walking along the street or waiting in line at the store into time spent with him, we are ushered into the presence of God for loving communion.

Matthew 6:9–13: "Pray then like this: Our Father in heaven, hallowed be your name. Your kingdom come, your will be done, on earth as it is in heaven. Give us this day our daily bread, and forgive us our debts, as we also have forgiven our debtors. And

lead us not into temptation, but deliver us from evil."

Jesus' disciples asked him to teach them to pray, and he obliged. "Heavenly Father" appears in the Old Testament, but calling him "our" Father meant that the disciples were invited into a familial relationship with each other and Jesus and into intimacy with the same Father. God's will, provision, forgiveness, and guidance sustain Christians as he advances his kingdom on earth, his ever-expanding reign in, through, and around us.

Matthew 7:7–11: "Ask, and it will be given to you; seek, and you will find; knock, and it will be opened to you. For everyone who asks receives, and the one who seeks finds, and to the one who knocks it will be opened. Or which one of you, if his son asks him for bread, will give him a stone? Or if he asks for a fish, will give him a serpent? If you then, who are evil, know how to give good gifts to your children, how much more will your Father who is in heaven give good things to those who ask him!"

Asking, seeking, and knocking are all metaphors of rising levels of intensity for prayer. God expects his people to make requests of him in prayer. He responds to the prayers of those who believe that "it will be given," "you will find," and the door "will be opened."

Matthew 26:39: "And going a little farther he fell on his face and prayed, saying, 'My Father, if it be possible, let this cup pass from me; nevertheless, not as I will, but as you will.'"

At the moment of Jesus' greatest temptation, he submitted to his Father's will. He would carry the punishment for all humanity's sin, and, even more grievous, he would experience abandonment from his Father. He let the Father have the last word.

Luke 18:1–8:

And he told them a parable to the effect that they ought always to pray and not lose heart. He said, "In a certain city there was a judge who neither feared God nor

respected man. And there was a widow in that city who kept coming to him and saying, 'Give me justice against my adversary.' For a while he refused, but afterward he said to himself, 'Though I neither fear God nor respect man, yet because this widow keeps bothering me, I will give her justice, so that she will not beat me down by her continual coming.'" And the Lord said, "Hear what the unrighteous judge says. And will not God give justice to his elect, who cry to him day and night? Will he delay long over them? I tell you, he will give justice to them speedily. Nevertheless, when the Son of Man comes, will he find faith on earth?"

This widow—destitute, defenseless, powerless, and in the ultimate state of vulnerability and need—with no one to represent her, presented herself before an unrighteous judge who had failed to administer God's just ways toward the oppressed. Her steely, squeaky-wheel-gets-the-grease determination resulted in the judge resigning to her request. He may have been unjust, but he was not dumb. If he continued to refuse, she would continue to request. The insensitive judge responded to the persistence of one he did not know or care about. How much more will a righteous God respond to his children? Always pray and never give up. The goal is not to get what we want, but to get what God wants: honor given to his name and love for his people.

John 14:13–14: "Whatever you ask in my name, this I will do, that the Father may be glorified in the Son. If you ask me anything in my name, I will do it."

We need to understand that adding "In Jesus' name" to the end of our prayers is not some magical, formulaic postscript, boosting the probability of a desired outcome. To pray in Jesus' name means praying in harmony with God's character and desires as revealed in his Word. Elsewhere (1 John 5:14–15) John assured Christians that their prayers are heard. Regardless of outcome,

Christians are to be faithful and patient in prayer, obedient and submissive to God's response.

Romans 8:26–27: "Likewise the Spirit helps us in our weakness. For we do not know what to pray for as we ought, but the Spirit himself intercedes for us with groanings too deep for words. And he who searches hearts knows what is the mind of the Spirit, because the Spirit intercedes for the saints according to the will of God."

Our prayers can be plagued with the inability to know specifically what and how to pray. Aware of this, God's Holy Spirit is there to step in. He bears our burdens along with us on our behalf as a divine advocate with his wordless groans. God, who searches hearts, and his Spirit are united in purpose to accomplish God's will through the power of prayer.

Ephesians 6:13–18:

Therefore take up the whole armor of God, that you may be able to withstand in the evil day, and having done all, to stand firm. Stand therefore, having fastened on the belt of truth, and having put on the breastplate of righteousness, and, as shoes for your feet, having put on the readiness given by the gospel of peace. In all circumstances take up the shield of faith, with which you can extinguish all the flaming darts of the evil one; and take the helmet of salvation, and the sword of the Spirit, which is the word of God, praying at all times in the Spirit, with all prayer and supplication. To that end keep alert with all perseverance, making supplication for all the saints.

Paul, who began his letter to the Ephesians with the language of power and principalities, concluded it with the language of weapons for warfare. The armor, consisting of the six vital pieces, expresses dependence on God. Alert prayer is to be done all the

time, in varied forms, with all perseverance, and for all the saints if we have any hope at all to stand firm and advance against the powers of darkness.

Philippians 4:6: "Do not be anxious about anything, but in everything by prayer and supplication with thanksgiving let your requests be made known to God."

God knows the harmful effects of worry on our bodies and souls. The world won't understand his antidote, yet believers will: pray, ask, and give thanks. If our God is small, we have every right to worry. But if he is the one described in his Word, we must relinquish that right. Our confidence and ability to refrain from worry are grounded not in our own abilities, luck, or fate, but in the One who created time and sees and knows all things and outcomes. The way to be anxious for nothing is to be expectantly prayerful about everything.

Hebrews 10:19–22: "Therefore, brothers, since we have confidence to enter the holy places by the blood of Jesus, by the new and living way that he opened for us through the curtain, that is, through his flesh, and since we have a great priest over the house of God, let us draw near with a true heart in full assurance of faith, with our hearts sprinkled clean from an evil conscience and our bodies washed with pure water."

What follows "therefore" is the most appropriate response to the access believers have been given to come into the presence of God through the work (death) of Christ, the Great High Priest— we can draw near. We can bring the openness and transparency of a cleansed heart that is grounded in confident trust of what Christ's saving work has already done in our lives.

Food for Thought

It is easy to be confused by the labeling of different kinds of prayer. There are brief breath prayers, focused contemplative prayers,

and conversational prayers—just to name a few. The kind of prayer that encompasses all the types is the one that requires the diligence, brokenness, and willingness of the one praying to be transformed by God.

Prayer is not only concerned with the well-being of the one who prays but also with a desire for the will of God to be done and for glory and honor to be brought to his name. I can approach God in anger, in want, in frustration, or in praise. He is big enough to take it all, and I am changed as I leave the time with God in prayer. Praying indicates I am genuinely convinced of his wisdom, love, goodness, and power. Prayer is a humbling process that takes place over time.

My husband and I were married for over thirty years when his mother was diagnosed with lung cancer. Norm became a Christian as an adult and is the only Christian in his family, so far. Sometimes this created difficult family situations. Seemingly, as our relationship with Christ grew, so did his family's resentment. The most difficult relationship existed between my mother-in-law and me. Criticisms and demeaning remarks became an expected part of our visits to their home.

I often asked God why he would give me a mother-in-law who didn't care about me. I tried letting her comments and criticisms "roll off my back," but to no avail. If anything, her remarks were like barbed hooks that tore at my heart.

For years I would take this to God in prayer. I prayed for her salvation, for the right heart attitude and words to say to her, and for the strength to love her. I prayed for the reminder of his love for me. There were times when prayer didn't seem to work. Disappointment with her and disappointment in God made me wonder if my prayers for our relationship had fallen on deaf ears and into powerless hands. I grew tired of praying for her and would confess that I had no love for her. Nearly three decades of riding on this roller coaster of dutiful love for God, rationalized ambivalence, self-preservation, and hopelessness came to a strong

corrective at the end of 2006. My mother-in-law's diagnosis of cancer required her to have frequent doctor's appointments, which her husband faithfully attended with her.

One morning as I sat in my prayer chair in our living room, reading my Bible, God redirected my attention to thoughts of my mother-in-law. With his gentle voice, he asked me to call my mother-in-law. At first I discounted it as something I must have been imagining. When I sensed the same request again, I refused with, "I am sitting here reading your Word. Wouldn't you rather me do that?" His request came again. Reluctantly I got up out of my chair and walked all the way to the kitchen (all of twenty-three steps) to call her. I anticipated leaving a voice message.

She was almost out the door for her doctor's appointment when her phone rang. To my surprise, she answered. After a brief greeting, she asked why I called. My answer was, "I just wanted to tell you that I love you." I was not ready for her reply. "I love you, too." That was it and that was enough. Words I never thought I would hear were said. Decades of sadness and regret were beginning to be redeemed. He had heard my prayer.

Two weeks before her death, her decline seemed particularly marked, as her physical body deteriorated from the cancer ravaging within her. She was able to respond only with nods of her head and a periodic wave of her hand. I made it a point to touch her, speak loudly into her ear, stroke her hand, and kiss her.

On the evening of Easter 2007, my husband and children surrounded her and shared the gospel message with her. God had cleared the room of any disruption that could impair her ability to hear this message. Each of us played a part—reciting a psalm or a passage, telling her of the love of God and the reason for Easter. Our daughter, Cami, explained the gospel and invited her to respond by squeezing her hand. I don't believe Cami had ever received a more meaningful, life-changing squeeze. Three days later, my mother-in-love was ushered into the presence of God, where she was able to see firsthand his glorious majesty. I cannot help but

think that she must have been amazed to finally discover that what her son's family had believed about God is actually true.

Prayer has that effect: proving God is real.

How To

Know that God always initiates. He invites men and women to keep company with him. Developing a relationship with us is God's goal, and answers to prayer are a means he uses to foster self-disclosure, growth, and understanding of both him and ourselves. It matters far less how, when, and what we say than how well we know the One we pray to. Reading books and articles on prayer are helpful, but prayer can best be learned by actually praying. Theory and practice are two halves of the whole. We learn what we practice. Start by praying briefly and often. Praying aloud when we are alone familiarizes us with the sound of praying from the heart.

The acrostic A-C-T-S is a helpful tool to guide prayer. We can begin with *Adoration*, worshiping him by recognizing aspects of his character, his attributes. *Confession* is acknowledging the chasm that exists between us and God, recognizing that sin is anything that gets in the way of a reconciled relationship with God or with others. Anything. *Thanksgiving* reminds us that God is the giver of everything and the one we are completely dependent on. Giving thanks to him reveals our dependent heart. Perhaps the most frequented element of prayer, and sometimes the only part we pray, is *Supplication*, asking for things.

Yes, we are told to bring our requests to God and that he delights in giving gifts to his children (Matthew 7:7–11). Perhaps it's our selfish nature, our culture, or how we have learned to pray, but if we believe prayer to be primarily a way to receive what we ask for, God simply becomes our own personal Santa Claus. We climb up on his lap, hand him our wish list of wants, and expect him to fill the list. If God's answer is not what we asked for or expected, prayer is deemed unworthy of our time, energy,

or emotion. We become people more concerned with how God is serving us than how we are serving him.

Try spending a few moments in following the A-C-T-S guide—but don't pray the S; in other words, don't ask for anything. Observe what your prayers are like. You may discover your relationship with God is based on your asking and his giving. Any one-sided conversation that is focused on asking for things reveals a friendship based on receiving. When more attention is focused on the A, C, and T, there is a heightened affirmation of God's presence, power, care, and involvement. Subsequently, supplications become fewer and less pressing. Let this periodic exercise impact your regular prayer life. C. S. Lewis wrote, "Gratitude exclaims, very properly, 'How good of God to give me this.' Adoration says, 'What must be the quality of that Being whose far-off and momentary coruscations are like this!' One's mind runs back up the sunbeam to the sun."[1]

Prayer is essential to a deepening relationship with God. It is the one act on which all other spiritual exercises depend. Silence and solitude without prayer are empty aloneness. Reading the Bible without prayer is a vain attempt to know God. Meditation without prayer is powerless deep thinking. If you have spent time in prayer and it has not impacted your relationship with God and others, then you have just been talking to yourself.

Pitfalls

Acquiring Things

If the primary reason we pray is to acquire things, God becomes someone who exists to serve us. Truncating prayer to simply asking and receiving ignores God's relational purpose in our engaging him in dialogue. Living in an affluent society compounds this materialistic view; we just buy what we "need" instead of trusting God for discernment of our needs versus wants. This further reduces the need for prayer and submission to God.

Waste of Time

Many protest, "Why waste time praying if God knows what I need anyway?" Yes, God knows our every need and every word we will say, but he wants us to pray because of what happens when we do. It is in the process of praying that our relationship with God is deepened. When we fail to be in prayer to God, we are more inclined to attribute events to fate or destiny; and this contributes nothing to building faith in an omnipotent, powerful, intimate God.

Nowhere in Scripture does God even imply that prayer is in any way a waste of time. In fact, it's quite the opposite: there is much need, incredible power, and always an answer to prayer. Only in Western logic do we respond to God's omniscience by not telling him anything. Jesus said that because God knows everything, we can tell him anything. His omniscience brings limitless freedom in communication. He often gives his children the impulse and ability to pray in order that he might respond to their petitions and carry out aspects of his will. A cultivated rhythm of refusing to respond to God's initiatives breeds fear and laziness in us. We have a formidable enemy whose strategy focuses on keeping us from praying.

Minimizing

When saying grace is reduced to the penalty for being the last one to arrive at a table meal, we have failed to realize that drudgery and holiness, busyness and God's presence, dullness and power, selfish ignorance and infinite wisdom have nothing in common.

God's Stirring

Even the smallest of steps in praying lead to wanting to pray more. The communion with the God of all creation, as he invites us to join him in holy moments, is beyond compare. Just to sense his good pleasure in our responding to his invitation to "come" draws us more frequently to him. Even our distractions in prayer, as we follow those "rabbit trails," can be fuel for discovering the very hindrances that become interrupting static in our conversations with God.

Reflections from the Heart

- It was quite a different experience praying with God through the adoration, confession, and thanksgiving, while leaving out the supplication. I felt embarrassed that after all this time I hadn't seen how selfish I was when praying to God. It brought out things in my heart that I normally would have passed up talking to God about because I would be asking God for help in some area or questioning why he had not yet answered my questions. It was awesome to see how much God had to say when I was listening. *Sarah C.*

- For years my Sunday Christian life has portrayed prayer as a boring, tedious, and largely useless practice. This was even more-so emphasized by prayer becoming a punishment for tardy people. In the midst of all this antiprayer propaganda, it's not overly difficult to imagine why the purpose of prayer became perverted in my life. *Jonathan K.*

- Today I came before the Lord in prayer. Doing so was a very awkward but also amazing experience. I must confess that I have not been praying to the Lord nearly as much as I should, partly because I often feel as though I don't have the time, but also because I feel inadequate and uncertain as I pray. Thus reading and learning about prayer this week has been very convicting and also encouraging as I begin to learn how to pray. *Chelsea G.*

- As I adored God and simply stated who he is, I found myself shocked. I had never done that before. Always, I praised and honored God through giving thanks, and never by stating who he is. I can remember my reaction the first time this

week I stated, "You are God, and more powerful than anything I can comprehend." I found myself lifted into a place of worship almost immediately, because I had subjected myself to his being and did not come with the slightest inclination to ask for anything or remember what he has done for me. My prayer was about him, and I have found this week that this realignment in my prayers has been relieving and encouraging, uplifting me by opening my heart and mind to rely on him because he alone can provide. . . . The basic act of stating who God is, as King, Ruler, as the God omniscient, omnipresent, omnipotent, put me in a place of security because I knew that he cares for me and loves me as the Creator. Because I opened my communication with this clarification of his being, I became settled in the rest of my prayer and approach. *Micah Y.*

- Praying using the A-C-T-S acronym was something I found to be quite challenging. Although we were instructed to leave out the S for this week, I kept catching myself going straight to it in my prayers. It was a wonderful realization on how much I am always asking God for him to work in my life. I don't spend nearly the same amount of time just adoring God and praising him for who he is. Out of the letters in the acronym, I think I need to do more of the A and C. My pride keeps me from seeing how much I sin against God daily, and I pray that God would help me see it so I can confess to him and repent of it. But moreover, I hardly ever just sit in God's presence and adore him. I looked up the verb "adore" in the dictionary, and its definition was "to love and respect someone deeply." It comes from the Latin word *adorare*, which actually means worship. Worship is what we were made for and should thus manifest itself in my prayer time. *Erik A.*

Fill in the Blank

Prayer breaks the seduction of _____ and allows me to hear God's invitation to/for _____.

Closing Thought

Prayer is the pulse of an abiding life. It is vital and a vital sign. This gracious gift of speaking with and listening to God is brought to you on behalf of Jesus. He showed us the importance of praying by praying.

Helpful Reads

Richard Foster, *Celebration of Discipline: The Path to Spiritual Growth* (San Francisco: HarperSanFrancisco, 1998), chapter 3.

Henry Holloman, *The Forgotten Blessing* (Nashville: Word Publishing, 1999), chapter 12.

Klaus Issler, *Wasting Time with God: A Christian Spirituality of Friendship with God* (Downers Grove: InterVarsity Press, 2001), chapters 6 and 8.

John Ortberg, *The Life You've Always Wanted: Spiritual Disciplines for Ordinary People* (Grand Rapids: Zondervan, 2004), chapter 6.

Donald Whitney, *Spiritual Disciplines for the Christian Life* (Colorado Springs: NavPress, 1991), chapter 4.

Dallas Willard, *The Spirit of the Disciplines: Understanding How God Changes Lives* (San Francisco: HarperSanFrancisco, 1991), 184–186.

Some Books on Prayer

Larry Crabb, *The PAPA Prayer: Discover the Sound of Your Father's Voice* (Nashville: Integrity Publisher, 2006).

Richard Foster, *Prayer: Finding the Heart's True Home* (San Francisco: HarperSanFrancisco, 1992).

W. Bingham Hunter, *The God Who Hears* (Downers Grove: InterVarsity Press, 1986).

Richard Peace, *Meditative Prayer: Entering God's Presence* (Colorado Springs: NavPress, 1998).

6
CONFESSION:
THE HUNCHBACK IN US ALL

Definition: Confession is that point when my mouth gives voice to what my heart knows to be true about my sin, no matter what the reason or cause, and without excuse. Genuine confession and repentance allow the soul to be most receptive to abundant, divine, life-transforming forgiveness.

Letting the Word Speak

Old Testament

Proverbs 28:13: "Whoever conceals his transgressions will not prosper, but he who confesses and forsakes them will obtain mercy."

True confession is characterized by a 180-degree turn in us (ב) with accompanying mercy and blessing from God. As part of the Wisdom Literature genre, these proverbial sayings describe wise principles rather than specific promises. These principles show us how to live life God's way. Here the writer exposed humanity's common sins and their common results. Concealed sin leaves guilt unaffected. Sin breaks the intimate familiarity God wants to have with us. When we acknowledge before God that our sin is sin and that we genuinely don't want to follow its path any longer, we receive mercy, a pardon, instead of getting what we

expect—punishment. A pardon from God is unlike anything else you can experience on earth. It reaches the uttermost crevices of the soul—bringing the freedom to live abundantly.

Psalm 51:1–6:

Have mercy on me, O God,
  according to your steadfast love;
according to your abundant mercy
  blot out my transgressions.
Wash me thoroughly from my iniquity,
  and cleanse me from my sin!
For I know my transgressions,
  and my sin is ever before me.
Against you, you only, have I sinned
  and done what is evil in your sight,
so that you may be justified in your words
  and blameless in your judgment.
Behold, I was brought forth in iniquity,
  and in sin did my mother conceive me.
Behold, you delight in truth in the inward being,
  and you teach me wisdom in the secret heart.

In the Psalms we find a beautiful blend of sound theology—right thoughts about God—and raw human emotion and experience. Suffering, disappointment, struggles, and distress launch the emotions that were penned in this lament psalm. Like wet clothing that clings to us, the accusing presence of David's ominous sin plagued him, and he acknowledged its pollution. (For more on his story and transformation, see 2 Samuel 11 and 12.) David knew that his sin went beyond his behavior and originated in his character. He cried out in an appeal to the God he knew to be loving and compassionate. It was from that love that God promised to forgive and cleanse David to the depths of his soul. David knew that his soul needed renewing and that he was dependent on God's truth and wisdom to cleanse his heart.

Psalm 139:23–24: "Search me, O God, and know my heart! Try me and know my thoughts! And see if there be any grievous way in me, and lead me in the way everlasting!"

The psalmist gave God free rein to go through every recess of his heart. He wanted to be purged of anything that might get in the way of their relationship. Self-examination is difficult. The psalmist knew he was in need of spiritual illumination to reveal his sins, and he was unwilling to listen to his own deceitfulness that had led him to believe he was "not really that bad." There is the way of vanity, sluggishness, worldliness, unbelief, and disobedience. And then there is God's way.

New Testament

Luke 15:17–32:

> But when he came to himself, he said, "How many of my father's hired servants have more than enough bread, but I perish here with hunger! I will arise and go to my father, and I will say to him, 'Father, I have sinned against heaven and before you. I am no longer worthy to be called your son. Treat me as one of your hired servants.'" And he arose and came to his father. But while he was still a long way off, his father saw him and felt compassion, and ran and embraced him and kissed him. And the son said to him, "Father, I have sinned against heaven and before you. I am no longer worthy to be called your son." But the father said to his servants, "Bring quickly the best robe, and put it on him, and put a ring on his hand, and shoes on his feet. And bring the fattened calf and kill it, and let us eat and celebrate. For this my son was dead, and is alive again; he was lost, and is found." And they began to celebrate.

Jesus' parables are infused with truth. This parable reveals the

truth of what God the Father and life in his kingdom are like. We have all been prodigal sons and daughters who have broken the Father's heart. In seeking to do things our own way, we prodigals squander much. We hope that we come to our senses and want to return home.

Regret and fear must have replayed in the son's mind countless times and perhaps even colored his anticipated response from his father. He was readied for his father's words that would be nothing less than a severe and stinging rebuke. But he was in for a surprise. It seems it was characteristic for the father to gaze out into the distance, hoping for any glimpse of his son's return. Then one day he saw his son coming, and it sent him tearing across the terrain, breaking many cultural protocols for a man of great respect, wealth, and social status. He stopped at nothing until he could feel the tattered-clothed, undernourished body of his son in his arms.

The repentant son never did finish speaking his rehearsed lines before his father showered him with gifts of honor. What a celebration! What an incredibly forgiving father! The famous painter Rembrandt was himself a prodigal. Toward the end of his life, he realized and experienced the healing touch of the forgiving Father, so artfully depicted in *The Return of the Prodigal Son*.

If you want to know what the Father is like, count the number of times in Luke 15:11–32 he is mentioned or alluded to by either title or pronoun. (Even more instances show up when the original Greek verb forms are taken into account!) When the father ran to his son, he intercepted the shame any onlookers might have wanted to thrust on the prodigal. Just as this father took on the shame, Christ took on the shame of the cross for you and me. It was enough for the father to know his son had come home.

No matter what we've done or what our experiences with an earthly parent were like, the love and forgiveness of God our heavenly Father are perfect. Nothing is beyond the reach of this Father's forgiveness. Nothing. His forgiveness knows no bounds.

He's been on a relentless pursuit to persuade you of the absolute completeness of his forgiveness. It's time to come home.

James 5:15–16: "And the prayer of faith will save the one who is sick, and the Lord will raise him up. And if he has committed sins, he will be forgiven. Therefore, confess your sins to one another and pray for one another, that you may be healed. The prayer of a righteous person has great power as it is working."

The prescription for the healing that forgiveness brings is confession and prayer. God doesn't portion out forgiveness in increments; when you ask for it, you get it all. But we often gloss over these few words: "Confess your sins to one another." Confession is part of our individual times of prayer with God and is also a corporate activity that involves those we've hurt or offended and should be a normative part of a healthy, believing community. There's something freeing about giving voice to our confession and allowing the offended or a trusted other to hear those words. Real freedom awaits us on the other side of confession.

1 John 1:8–10: "If we say we have no sin, we deceive ourselves, and the truth is not in us. If we confess our sins, he is faithful and just to forgive us our sins and to cleanse us from all unrighteousness. If we say we have not sinned, we make him a liar, and his word is not in us."

To even think or say we are without sin or don't need forgiveness is evidence of self-deception. This form of deception is filled with guilt. But where the truth of God resides, guilt has no grip. Trying to convince ourselves that we don't need God's forgiveness is like saying we have absolutely no need of him; it is an assault to his truth that "all have sinned." The sense in which John penned the word *forgive* implies that God forgives daily. Complete forgiveness and divine pardon await us the moment we own our mistakes and messes and look to Christ for grace.

Food for Thought

I once asked God for a word that described our students. When he finally responded, he gave me a picture instead of a word. The picture was of a hunchback. Puzzled by the picture, I took a walk around campus and asked God, "Who are the hunchbacks?" and "Why are they so?" His answer? Unconfessed sin. I started to see the hunchback: the Hunchback of Unconfessed Sin.

I have an antique mirror hanging in the entry hall of our home. One day I noticed some darkened areas around the edges. After a number of phone calls, a mirror specialist diagnosed this as "silvering." I was told that moisture had seeped in between the layers of glass and that bacteria had caused the graying areas. Not only does this condition prevent any kind of reflection, but, if untreated, it would likely spread. Being told that the process of removing the silvering was quite expensive, I hung the mirror back up on the wall. That silvering is a picture of what sin is like in my life. It prevents me from reflecting the One who wants to shine through me. If left alone, it spreads. And it is expensive to remove; it cost Jesus his life.

Confession means locating myself honestly before God and, sometimes, before a trusted friend. My friend Kate approached me in the early weeks of our new friendship and asked me if we could get to the level of confession. "Of course!" I responded, while praying, "God, what did I just get myself into?" Kate and I met a week later, and our mutual confession became the watershed in our relationship. We were able to explore the depth of friendship in safety that God desires for his people. Years later, this same friendship continues.

Christians are called to suffer many things, but unconfessed sin isn't one of them. We were not designed to bear the weight of unconfessed sin. Jesus took care of that. Confession is important because forgiveness is critical. The two go hand in hand. Confession disarms the power of sin; forgiveness is armed with

the power of God. Together God uses them to transform us from burdened hunchbacks to freed saints.

How To

Sin is anything that gets in the way of a right relationship with God or with others. Blame shifting, faultfinding, and glossing over sin compromise the process of confession. Our confession of sin, owning our part in a thought, act, or relationship that dishonors God, moves us into agreement with God. The more specific we can be in confession, the more available we make ourselves to God's Spirit doing his work and the less alluring sin becomes.

The horizontal dimension of confession to another involves the one we have offended (if possible) or a trusted friend. Confession is a mark of a healthy community. Be prayerful about the person you confess to, and be alert to God's leading. If you are already in an established relationship with someone—preferably of the same gender—you might approach that person with a simple question: "Do you think we can get to the level of confession?" A true friend will sense the seriousness of the matter, be silent before you, will listen without judgment, and accept you—just as Jesus does. If you choose to take it to God alone, that's a great start. Just be open and obedient when he gently challenges you to approach another trusted soul.

Confession is the precursor of repentance. In agreeing with God about anything that displeases him, we take responsibility for the transgression. This leads to a change in attitude toward the offense. We begin to understand how ugly sin is and how much God hates it. Repentance involves both a change in attitude and a dependence on the power of God's Spirit to effect transformation. Confession and repentance without a forward-moving dependence on God can lead to a cycle of repeated confessions of diminishing returns. His way leads to healing and restoration. Being forgiven doesn't make us sinless, but it can make us sin less.

Fear

Fear keeps us from the freedom that awaits us in confessing sin. We try so hard at fashioning the image we want others to believe about us. The fear of anyone finding out our faults can stop us dead in our tracks. The fear of that person posting our confession on Facebook can be paralyzing. We've all been burned in a relationship where the confidentiality on a sensitive subject was broken. It hurts. But as you seek a trusted friend or mentor, don't allow fear to thwart your God-given need to be in healthy, transparent community.

Excuses

We do not like being wrong. Nobody does. Our ego finds confession problematic and will search for ways to avoid it. Excuses quickly appear: "Everybody does it"; "It wasn't a *big* sin"; "God, you don't understand how hurt I am"; "God already knows what I did and he'll forgive me"; "People won't like me if they really knew what I did." When we hide behind excuses, we keep ourselves from dealing with the fact that God hates sin. Evidence of his wrath against sin is seen at the cross, where his anger was satisfied in the sacrifice of his Son. Knowing and remembering who we are in Christ enable us to humbly approach a holy God, receive his grace and forgiveness, and live in freedom as forgiven souls.

Forgiving Myself

Some of us are convinced that we cannot forgive ourselves for some sin and find ourselves trapped in self-defeating guilt. This guilt need not be perpetuated. Instead, we all need to understand and experience the completeness of God's forgiveness. His forgiveness brings peace and cleansing from the guilt and shame. Forgiving ourselves brings none of these realities. We need the true forgiveness that only God can give. Confession begins the

process of growing in this truth and living out the satisfaction and fullness of his generous gift of forgiveness.

God's Stirring

Don't worry about surprising God with something he didn't already know. Our ability to be humble and honest before God parallels our ability to be honest and humble before others. Confession to God and to others grows in us humility that is God pleasing. When you confess to another, don't be surprised if those you confess to take the opportunity to confess something on their hearts to you. Seize the opportunity to be gracious and kind, extending Christlike forgiveness and acceptance of them. Forgiveness is critical because forgiven saints find it easier to forgive others.

Whether or not you experience an immediate difference, you can know with certainty that in Christ you are completely forgiven. Instead of getting hung up on "forgiving yourself," consider more intently the cost, depth, completeness, and finished work of Christ's sacrifice on the cross. God wants you to know you are completely forgiven.

Reflections from the Heart

• Why is confession so difficult for most people, including myself? It may be the fear of revealing who I really am, the upsetting task of telling loved ones where I have fallen short. It is so easy to build up a wall and not let others closer into the deeper issues of my heart. But the longer I pour lacquer over my faults and failures in a frantic attempt to cover over my sins, the more I feel hurt, discouraged, and alone. [This particular sin] is like a sticky amoeba that has leeched onto the softness of my skin, feeding from the flesh of my body. Every other part of me feels normal and healthy, but this one spot drains all the energy from me. I don't like it. I feel trapped,

but the more I pull and tear at it, the more of a mess it makes, clinging ever more tightly to my body. I cannot get it off and it suffocates me. What else can I do? Will others notice this ugly blotch? Maybe if I cover over it, no one will see. I hide it and they do not discover it, but now what? Now I am truly alone with no one to help. Now I can pretend it is not there. Maybe if I just go on with the rest of my life, no one will see how ugly this makes me. Maybe if I look long enough in the other direction, it will just disappear. Deep down I know that I cannot go on this way. It is eating me alive. *Alyssa M.*

- I have burdens that I have carried around for a while, which I have never been able to truly allow God to forgive me for. But I found that when I was able to share things that have been going on the past year and a half to a friend that I made a few weeks ago, it seemed as if God was speaking to me through my friend. . . . When I was able to break down those walls, confession really helped me see the acceptance of Christ. *Cody C.*

- Through confessing my actions to one of the leaders, and now one of my closest friends, I was able to let the Holy Spirit show me the cause of my actions. I yearned for love. I wanted it, and as God's creation, I needed it. Yet, I was searching in all the wrong places for it. Like many girls my age, I had fallen into the lie that true happiness was found in the arms of a man rather than in a trusting relationship with Christ. I had also learned that I had poor self-esteem in my thinking that I would never be good enough to one day have a wonderful husband who loved Christ more than he loved me. This view of myself had caused me to lower my standards for someone who did not even love God. Discovering the source of my actions has helped me to place both of my eyes on Christ for the first time in my life. . . . I never knew how difficultly simple the act of confession was. I was scared to confront the issues

in my life because I wanted to believe that I was perfect. Yet, God showed me how powerful he can be in the presence of a trusted friend. My act of confession has moved me forward in my relationship with Christ by allowing him to take control of my fears, worries, and thoughts. Trusting God with the future is unsettling at first because we do not know what it entails, yet doing this can bring so much freedom and beauty into one's life. I am still learning to trust in the One who created me. *Tiffany C.*

- During this means of grace I had a hard time putting into action what I felt God calling me to do. But I think that is because I had been ignoring God's call for a long time. As soon as I began the readings for this week, God gave me a person and that was my dad. I had confessed to God that I had allowed myself to stay distant from my father because that way I did not have to listen to what he had to say. At first it was so that he would not hurt me, but then later it became my way of revenge until the point where I wanted to turn back; I just didn't know how because it became pattern. As soon as my dad would start talking, I would put up a cold shield automatically, and it was as if I was someone else. I felt like I was watching someone else talk to my dad. I had confessed this to God and many other people, but for some reason I could not stop it. I realized that just confessing was not enough, and part of confession is changing the behavior. I began to talk to God about how I could possibly fix this problem. I did not want to have a hard heart toward my father any longer. I wanted to call him, but I still could not bring myself to do it. For my [project] I chose to interview my mom. I could not meet with her in person so I decided to help her set up a Skype account so we could talk that way. Just as we were finishing, my dad walked into the room. No one knew he would be home that day, so it was a surprise to everyone.

He sat down at the computer and we started to talk. I do not think I have had a real conversation with my dad in over a year. I felt God prompt me to go deeper. I asked him if he was busy next weekend because my boyfriend has a game on Saturday near home that I am coming up for and I wondered if he wanted to come. He said he had plans with my uncle and could not come, but he was thankful I invited him. God led me to ask him into a very personal part of my life because from the beginning I did not want my dad to be part of any of my relationships, but especially with a boyfriend. I walked away somewhat thankful that my dad could not come, but I trusted that God would grow our relationship in another way, and he did. The next day I got a text from my mom saying that my dad took the whole weekend off and changed his plans so that he could go to the game and hang out with the family. Confession without action is hardly confession at all, but when we confess with our actions, God will work in mighty ways beyond what we could ever fathom. *Mikaela F.*

- In these "rational lies" I foolishly and pridefully thought, "*I don't need to confess my sin to anyone else. After all, I've already told God and been forgiven. Why drag someone else into this mess?*" Thankfully, God helped me break through this foolish thinking and meet with Professor Delgado. I was nervous, scared, and every part of me seemed like it didn't want to confess. But I did it anyway. When I did confess, I found something that I did not expect: empathy and understanding. Before confessing, I had assumed that any revelation of my sins to someone else would result in condemnation and disapproval. However, when I practiced confession, I experienced just the opposite. Not only was Professor D. kind enough to listen to my story and sympathize with me, but he also provided me with concrete methods and guidance to stop this sin and grow in my Christian walk. All in all, practicing the means of grace

of confession enabled me to see and experience one very important spiritual truth: sin and evil often function like fungi, growing and contaminating in the dark. Confession, however, acts like the light that kills a fungus, and it is only when sin is confessed that one can be free from the burden of unrevealed sin. All in all, practicing this means of grace taught me that confession is a vital component in the life of a Christian, for it is only through confession that one may begin to be healed and restored. *Sam S.*

- As I lay there on the bed, whispering to her what I had held on to for so long, I emptied myself to her, laying everything out in the open. I knew she wouldn't look at me differently, but I now have nothing left to hold on to. I have given everything I have done to her, and she got to tell me that I'm forgiven and our relationship is better for it. I got to let thirteen years' worth of burdens go and release my pain. In response, she also confessed to me some things of her past, and although she has a much different upbringing than I do, because she came to Jesus at a later age, we shared the same desire to hold on to our sin. We discussed our false humility of holding on to our sin for ourselves. Whether it is doubting God's power of forgiveness or pride in our own sins, we both shared our deepest burdens and were forgiven. . . . Sharing this particular sin with another person has had some effects like flashbacks and old memories that have been difficult to deal with, but as I slowly accept my forgiveness, the condemnation is slowly fading. Confession has never been easy for me because my family and church do not talk about confession to others very often, but I definitely would like to participate in this means of grace more often. If I ask for God's forgiveness more, then maybe I will feel less condemnation and not let my sins sit within me for so long. *Danica O.*

Fill in the Blank

Confession breaks the seduction of _____ and allows me to hear God's invitation to/for _____.

Closing Thought

You may be hesitant to exercise confession, fearing what you believe God would say. Read Luke 15:1–32 again (and again) until you can begin to fathom that no matter how broken or compromised your life might be, nothing is beyond the reach of your Father's forgiveness, mercy, and love. Nothing. Others of you may be ready to take God's lead and confess to a trusted friend. Whichever way you choose, you don't have to be a hunchback anymore. Because Christ's work is completed, you are completely forgiven.

Helpful Reads

Richard Foster, *Celebration of Discipline: The Path to Spiritual Growth* (San Francisco: HarperSanFrancisco, 1998), chapter 10.

Klaus Issler, *Wasting Time with God: A Christian Spirituality of Friendship with God* (Downers Grove: InterVarsity Press, 2001), chapter 3.

John Ortberg, *The Life You've Always Wanted: Spiritual Disciplines for Ordinary People* (Grand Rapids: Zondervan, 2004), chapter 8.

Dallas Willard, *The Spirit of the Disciplines: Understanding How God Changes Lives* (San Francisco: HarperSanFrancisco, 1991), 187–189.

7
CONFERENCE:
A KIND OF PARADISE

Definition: The intentional conversation among a limited number of people in which they integrate their growing knowledge of the Bible with their concern for one another's soul. Emphasis is placed more on issues of the heart than on external behavior, for from the heart all expressions of life emerge.

Letting the Word Speak

After each of these verses that lend biblical support for conference, I have included an explanatory comment from an English Puritan.

Old Testament

Psalm 37:30: "The mouth of the righteous utters wisdom, and his tongue speaks justice."

A person whose heart is grounded in God's law speaks with wisdom that is superior to any the world has to offer.

> A gracious person hath not only Religion in his heart, but in his *tongue. The Law of God is in his heart, and his tongue talketh of Judgement*: he drops holy words as Pearls. 'Tis the fault of Christians, that they do not in company provoke themselves to set good discourse on foot:

it is a sinfull modesty: there is much visiting, but they do not give one another's souls a visit. In worldly things their tongue is *as a Pen of a ready Writer*; but in matters of Religion, they are as if their tongue *did cleave to the roof of their mouth*. As we must answer to God for *idle words*; so for *sinfull* silence.[1]

Psalm 66:16: "Come and hear, all you who fear God, and I will tell what he has done for my soul."

Found in the thanksgiving portion of a hymn of descriptive praise, the psalmist entreats "all . . . who fear God," which included Israelites and believers from other nations, to witness his words of testimony of God's gracious deliverance.

"Thus [Christians] when you meet, give one anothers Souls a visit, drop your Knowledge, impart your experiences each to other."[2]

Psalm 119:11–13: "I have stored up your word in my heart, that I might not sin against you. Blessed are you, O LORD; teach me your statutes! With my lips I declare all the rules of your mouth."

The Christian is to speak the Word of God to others. Our speech mirrors the stirrings of the heart.

"[The psalmist] telleth us, that if we will speak profitably unto others, we must first have the word within us; and that not lightly floating in our brain, but deeply setled and hidden in our hearts."[3]

Proverbs 27:17: "Iron sharpens iron, and one man sharpens another."

This kind of sharpening means the interaction between friends that effects a positive change in personality or character.

"In naturall things man standeth in neede of helpe, then much more in spirituall things he standeth in neede of others. And as *iron sharpeneth iron, so one friend another*, Pro.27. And as two

eies see more, two eares heare more, and two hands can doe more than one, so this is a speciall communion of Saints."[4]

Malachi 3:16: "Then those who feared the Lord spoke with one another. The Lord paid attention and heard them, and a book of remembrance was written before him of those who feared the Lord and esteemed his name."

The Puritans frequently cited this passage to support holy conference. As you read the comments below, sense the passion they had for the purposes and benefits God intended for this practice. Evidence that this passion continued beyond the Puritan era is revealed in the following quote from Matthew Henry's (1662–1714) commentary on this verse.

> They *spoke often to one another* concerning the God they feared, and that name of his which they thought so much of; for out of the abundance of the heart the mouth will speak, and a good man, out of a *good treasure* there, will *bring forth good things. Those that feared the Lord* kept together as those that were company for each other; they spoke kindly and endearingly one to another, for the preserving and promoting of mutual love, that that might not *wax cold* when *iniquity* did thus *abound*. They spoke intelligently and edifyingly to one another, for the increasing and improving of faith and holiness; they *spoke one to another* in the language of those that fear the Lord and think on his name—the language of Canaan. When profaneness had come to so great a height as to trample upon all that is sacred, then those that feared the Lord *spoke often one to another*.
>
> He took notice of their pious discourses, and was graciously present at their conferences: . . . The gracious God observes all the gracious words that proceed out of the mouths of his people; they need not desire that men may hear them, and commend them; let

them not seek praise from men by them, nor affect to be taken notice of by them; but let it satisfy them that, be the conference ever so private, God sees and hears in secret and will *reward openly*. When the two disciples, going to Emmaus, were discoursing concerning Christ, he hearkened and heard, and joined himself to them, and made a third.

He kept an account of them. . . . Not that the Eternal Mind needs to be reminded of things by book and writings, but it is an expression after the manner of men, intimating that their pious affections and performances are kept in remembrance as punctually and particularly as if they were written in a book, as if journals were kept of all their conferences. . . . Never was any good word spoken of God, or for God, from an honest heart, but it was registered, that it might be recompensed in the resurrection of the just, and in no wise lose its reward.[5]

New Testament

Mark 4:10: "And when he was alone, those around him with the twelve asked him about the parables."

The Gospels give evidence of Jesus personally exercising conference with his disciples. He is found to be conferring with his disciples and the rest of his hearers, "opening" or explaining many parables to them.

"You will find that most of the preaching recorded in the New Testament, was by conference, and frequently interlocutory, and that with one or two, fewer or more, as opportunity served. Thus Christ himself did most commonly preach."[6]

Luke 24:15, 32: "While they were talking and discussing together, Jesus himself drew near and went with them. . . . They said to each other, 'Did not our hearts burn

Knowing Grace

within us while he talked to us on the road, while he opened to us the Scriptures?'"

Further support for conference is derived from Jesus' postresurrection appearance to the two disciples as they walked along the road to Emmaus and communed over the death and sufferings of Christ. This encounter served as evidence that by holy discourse Jesus drew near and accompanied them. Holy discourse brings Christ into our company, which in turn enables believers to resemble Christ more closely.

"While they communed together, Jesus himself drew near, and went with them. When men entertain bad discourse, Satan draws near, and he makes one of the company; but when they have holy and gracious conference, Jesus Christ draws near, and where-ever he comes, he brings a blessing along with him."[7]

"We see the poore Disciples, when they were in a damp for the losse of Christ, after he comes, meets them, and talks of holy things. In that very conference *their hearts were warmed and kindled*: For, next to Heaven it selfe our meeting together here, it is a kinde of Paradise, the greatest pleasure of the world is, to meet with those here, whom we shall ever live with in Heaven."[8]

Romans 14:1: "As for the one who is weak in faith, welcome him, but not to quarrel over opinions."

The mutual benefits of godly conference are to be the substitute for the divisiveness caused by the arguing and quarreling instigated by more mature believers with those younger in the faith.

> The third meanes is holy conference with our godly brethren; for hereby those which are falling are confirmed, and the wearie hands and weake knees strengthened, as *Eliphas* speaketh, *Job* 43.4 And those who are weake in faith are comforted and established with the godly instructions, profitable exhortations and sweet consolations of those who are more strong. And

therefore the Apostle *Paul* exhorts those who had attained unto a great measure of faith, that they admit such as were weake into their company to be made partakers of their Christian conferences, to the end that hereby they might be more and more strengthened and confirmed.[9]

Ephesians 4:29: "Let no corrupting talk come out of your mouths, but only such as is good for building up, as fits the occasion, that it may give grace to those who hear."

Our speech to one another in godly consideration for the other will build both healthy and harmonious community and defeat Satan's aim to cause discord from within.

"The Apostle bids us *edifie one another, Ephes* 4.29. And how more than this way? Good conference enlightens the mind when it is ignorant; warms it when it is frozen; settles it when it is wavering. A good life adorns Religion; good discourse propagates it."[10]

Colossians 3:16: "Let the word of Christ dwell in you richly, teaching and admonishing one another in all wisdom, singing psalms and hymns and spiritual songs, with thankfulness in your hearts to God."

Paul desired for the church to engage in conference. This is to be a community-building affair where the natural expression of the church's growth in the knowledge of Christ appears in the words believers speak to one another.

"[Paul] willeth them to conferre of the Scriptures, to the profit of one another, so he sheweth them how they shall come unto it."[11]

Food for Thought

Between ancient and recent church history lies an often overlooked period of time when great authority was given to the words of Scripture and when growing in faith was accomplished in community. The words of the Bible became the litmus test for authentic and devoted lives. Weighing life against anything else was futile and led to a preoccupation with self and thus a meaningless existence. This characterizes the English Puritans of the sixteenth and seventeenth centuries.

Christian and Hopeful—protagonists in John Bunyan's (1628–1688) *Pilgrim's Progress*—discuss the plight of believers who backslide from faith. Christian's response includes the lack of conference as a cause of such spiritual decline: "They shun the company of lively and warm Christians"; and "After that they grow cold to public duty, as hearing, reading, godly conference, and the like." Godly conference is identified here as a profitable discipline whose neglect leads to a compromise in spiritual wellness.

Bunyan himself recalled a group of poor women sitting at a sunny doorway and conversing about the things of God: "*I heard, but I understood not* for they were far above out of my reach, for their talk was about a new birth, the work of God on their hearts, also how they were convinced of their miserable state by nature: they talked how God had visited their souls with his love in the Lord Jesus, and with what words and promises they had been refreshed, comforted, and supported, against the temptations of the Devil."[12]

Bunyan found something new and confessed, "They were to me as if they had found a new world."[13] His subsequent times in meeting and conversing with these women stirred the questioning of his own soul and prompted godly meditation.

Pastors conferenced with other pastors and their congregants on matters of Scripture and of the soul. Parishioners conferenced with their peers, heads of households with all those living under their care, and parents with their children. Serendipitous conversations were often interjected with the language of biblical truth and soul care. And when face-to-face encounters were not possible, letters were written expressing the same deep level of concern for biblical truth and attentiveness to the heart.

Time and distance did not diminish the desire to foster soul care and biblical knowledge. A portion of a letter from Jonathan Michel pictures this desire:

> But yet considering some passages in your last and former Letters concerning your Spiritual Condition, and knowing by experience in my self the reality of such Complaints, I would not be so graceless as to neglect you wholly therein: And though I can say or do very little, yet a word or two might be of some use; nor do I know what guilt might lye upon me, if I should be silent or slight in this Case! And therefore [Dear ——] if my barren heart would suffer me, I would present you with a few words, as if you and I were alone in a Corner in the presence of God.[14]

The ease of spiritual drift, of losing track of the "true north" of biblical knowledge and spiritual growth, can be remedied by godly conference. Stepping out from the archives, we cannot help observing the delight and "paradise" that were intended to be employed and enjoyed in conference. We take with us an affirmation of the need for the experience of this manner of community and the idea that it can happen.

How To

Key to the exercise of conference is the desire to know God's Word better and to live out its truth. Well-formatted questions applied to a sermon message or Bible passage can further our understanding and application of Scripture. This may require advancing from questions with one-word answers to study questions that require deeper thought and discussion.

Here are a few typical questions the Puritans found useful in conference, redesigned for our contemporary understanding:

- What does God want you to know about him? About yourself?

- For what is the soul thankful?
- What are the words or actions that demonstrate your soul's love for Christ?
- What is your soul afraid of God knowing?
- To what extent is your soul willing to go to preserve unity in your community?

Consider asking these types of questions and, more importantly, answering them with an attentiveness to your own heart and the hearts of others. Be ready to experience a greater commitment to doing deeper life together in Christian community.

Pitfalls

Individualism

With the pervasive individualism that has permeated American culture, it is no wonder that authentic spiritual transformation fostered in community is threatened. Any disclosures of hurts, doubts, or weaknesses are usually reserved for a select few, if any at all. We are expected to "go it alone." Spiritually speaking, individualism is a detrimental mode of functioning.

Isolationism

Many of us live with overcrowded, conflicting, and unrelenting schedules. The residue effect of this, according to Lynn Smith-Lovin and Miller McPherson, sociologists at Duke University and the University of Arizona, is social isolation.[15] Their findings show many more Americans are completely isolated from those they might discuss important matters with. Dallas Willard warned that even members in a small group can become people adept at functioning in "well-calculated distance."[16] It may take a year just to get to the level of feeling safe and secure enough to share inward struggles, knowing you will still be accepted as you are but with the hope and desire to be transformed.

God's Stirring

Excitement about growing in Christlikeness is characteristic of those in a community that brings personal struggles honestly before one another and God. There is a connectedness that can be described as devoted friends who are "in your face and by your side." Gracious glimpses of godly transformation appear, causing a deeper humility and dependence on God. To see a powerful and loving God use his words of life to transform souls, marriages, workplace relationships, and family ties to impact the world creates a greater hunger and thirst for more of him.

Reflections from the Heart

- I have found a lot of comfort in talking about God and praying with other believers. A lot of times they bring different views that I have not looked at before. They are also the ones who have come to me when they think that I'm not doing right in an area in my life. It is hard to hear sometimes, but I am thankful, because they are looking after my soul with me. *Molly W.*

- We live in a very individualistic society, so much so that we never ask how our brother is doing spiritually. . . . Christians are not tapping the potential this powerful tool offers. . . . I realized the need for conferencing in my own life. It is very easy to deny, or simply forget, the role of Christian experience and growth. *Eric H.*

- Conference certainly is something of a lost art in this day and age. Very rarely did my family talk about a sermon heard on Sunday morning for any length of time. Usually it was largely superficial, general comments, without much thought afterwards, but I believe it has much to do with our passive culture. We like to be entertained, if the prevalence of TV and movies is any indication. We enjoy sitting back, watching

others' song and dance play out, and then getting up and going on with our lives, not giving much of a second thought to anything we see or hear. There is certainly a challenge to delving into Christian truths and carefully studying them with others. It requires work and discipline, but ultimately leads to a stronger faith. *Thomas M.*

- Conferencing involves confirming each other in faith and obedience and is more than just accountability partners. Growing up in a high school small group, I experienced accountability partners. It was interesting looking back on that because it did not really seem to affect my behavior or my disobedience because I would choose what I told them and leave out anything that I chose to keep private. *Kristen A.*

- What I truly looked forward to each week was meeting with my conference group every Friday because we were able to discuss what God had spoken to each of us through our readings. . . . I was fortunate to have a conference group that was so open with their feelings, and through that it caused me to be more open as well. *Ralph M.*

- Conferencing seems to be a missing link in our churches. It is where the private means of grace meets the public. In the evangelical world today we have a very strong emphasis on healing and redemption. However, the manner in which we carry that out is very top down. The preacher preaches and the listeners listen. Conferencing provides mutual dependency on the body for growth. . . . Even though I grew up in Africa where application is a very public practice, I have become quite individualistic in my faith. Thinking back now I have grown most in my faith and walk when I discussed deep spiritual matters with others. *Luke P.*

- The practice of the spiritual discipline of conference breaks the barriers of secrecy and loneliness and makes room for the

body of Christ to do what it is called to do, and that is love.
Paige W.

Fill in the Blank

Conference breaks the seduction of _____ and allows me to hear God's invitation to/for _____.

Closing Thought

In good company and conference the goodness of God and the struggles of life meet in loving acceptance and godly direction. This centuries-old practice, whose roots are found in Scripture, will foster community as Christ followers long for keeping themselves and others within the compass of God's Word by their conversations—whether they be audible, in print, or even on a social-networking site.

Helpful Reads

Joanne Jung, *Godly Conversation: Rediscovering the Puritan Practice of Conference* (Grand Rapids: Reformation Heritage, 2011).

8 SUFFERING: THE SACRED NIGHT OF THE SOUL

Definition: The response to soul-rattling circumstances where God takes the little we know of him and purposes to grow our compassion quotient for others and the kind of intimate knowledge, trust, experience, and hope that is found only in his abiding presence.

Letting the Word Speak

Old Testament

Job 2:13: "And they sat with him on the ground seven days and seven nights, and no one spoke a word to him, for they saw that his suffering was very great."

God let Job's three friends go at it for three rounds as they tried to root out the sin that must have escaped Job's discerning eye, thus causing this tragedy. Each one aimed at "curing" Job. After all, good people don't suffer, right? Unknown to Job, his suffering was the crucible for proving the authenticity of his faith in a good God.

There was, though, something redeemable about the behavior of Job's friends. When they first arrived to visit Job and were unable to even recognize him in his suffering, they sat. And sat.

For seven days they sat with Job in silence. They exercised "Don't fix me" grace—the grace of recognizing that caring for someone doesn't mean curing him. They refrained from the temptation to be the hero by saying just the right word or offering the perfect advice to make everything all right. Physical presence and silence speak volumes to those who are suffering.

Psalm 13:

> How long, O LORD? Will you forget me forever?
>> How long will you hide your face from me?
> How long must I take counsel in my soul
>> and have sorrow in my heart all the day?
> How long shall my enemy be exalted over me?
>
> Consider and answer me, O LORD my God;
>> light up my eyes, lest I sleep the sleep of death,
> lest my enemy say, "I have prevailed over him,"
>> lest my foes rejoice because I am shaken.
>
> But I have trusted in your steadfast love;
>> my heart shall rejoice in your salvation.
> I will sing to the LORD,
>> because he has dealt bountifully with me.

This individual psalm of lament reflects feelings of abandonment and the deep-rooted questioning about God found throughout human history. In the first set of two verses, David expressed his despair and inner wrestling through a prolonged struggle; he was at the end of his rope. He questioned whether God's apparent silence would last "forever" because he saw no end in sight. The next two verses record his plea for God's attention and answer. The final two verses reveal David's recollection of God's goodness and the certainty of God's continued kindness—*hesed*. God's love toward Israel and David in the past assured David about trusting God in the present. David didn't see himself as causing God's abandonment, nor did he respond

with denying God's existence because of the abandonment he felt. David decided to wait. And though his waiting was filled with questions and appeals, he committed to trusting God in his suffering.

Psalm 88:

O LORD, God of my salvation;
> I cry out day and night before you.
Let my prayer come before you;
> incline your ear to my cry!

For my soul is full of troubles,
> and my life draws near to Sheol.
I am counted among those who go down to the pit;
> I am a man who has no strength,
like one set loose among the dead,
> like the slain that lie in the grave,
like those whom you remember no more,
> for they are cut off from your hand.
You have put me in the depths of the pit,
> in the regions dark and deep.
Your wrath lies heavy upon me,
> and you overwhelm me with all your waves.
Selah

You have caused my companions to shun me;
> you have made me a horror to them.
I am shut in so that I cannot escape;
> my eye grows dim through sorrow.
Every day I call upon you, O LORD;
> I spread out my hands to you.
Do you work wonders for the dead?
> Do the departed rise up to praise you? Selah
Is your steadfast love declared in the grave,
> or your faithfulness in Abaddon?

Are your wonders known in the darkness,
    or your righteousness in the land of
forgetfulness?

But I, O Lord, cry to you;
    in the morning my prayer comes before you.
O Lord, why do you cast my soul away?
        Why do you hide your face from me?
Afflicted and close to death from my youth up,
    I suffer your terrors; I am helpless.
Your wrath has swept over me;
    your dreadful assaults destroy me.
They surround me like a flood all day long;
    they close in on me together.
    You have caused my beloved and my friend to
shun me;
        my companions have become darkness.

Though another lament psalm, this one is the "darkest" of all the psalms. The psalmist feared abandonment from friends and God. He gave voice to the intense pain within and continued to cry out to the Lord who listens. Faith can be real amid uncertainty, confusion, and hopelessness.

Isaiah 42:2–3: "He will not cry aloud or lift up his voice, or make it heard in the street; a bruised reed he will not break, and a faintly burning wick he will not quench; he will faithfully bring forth justice."

Isaiah described the servant as king in several chapters (Isaiah 9; 11; 32), but here he revealed the king as a servant. This obedient and responsive servant is a light to the nations, bringing justice without the use of oppression. The violence men use to conquer contrasts with how the servant acts toward the oppressed and weak. He tenderly cares for those who are helpless.

Knowing Grace

New Testament

Matthew 5:11, 16: "Blessed are you when others revile you and persecute you and utter all kinds of evil against you falsely on my account. . . . In the same way, let your light shine before others, so that they may see your good works and give glory to your Father who is in heaven."

The worst this life has to offer is the closest a Christ follower will ever get to hell. Our suffering is a clear reminder of the deep longing for heaven we each have. If we can glorify God in suffering, we magnify his glory to others. When a Christian is found faithful through the crucible of suffering, God's nature is revealed. This experience is quite contrary to the world's fear and anger when any form of pain and suffering occurs.

John 15:18–21:

> If the world hates you, know that it has hated me before it hated you. If you were of the world, the world would love you as its own; but because you are not of the world, but I chose you out of the world, therefore the world hates you. Remember the word that I said to you: "A servant is not greater than his master." If they persecuted me, they will also persecute you. If they kept my word, they will also keep yours. But all these things they will do to you on account of my name, because they do not know him who sent me.

When, not if, opposition comes, be reminded of its root cause: your association with Jesus and the world's ignorance of God. Persecution shouldn't be a surprise, but rather expected. Devoted followers of Christ are to be known by their love, whereas the world will be known for its inevitable and continuing hatred of them.

John 16:33: "I have said these things to you, that in me you may have peace. In the world you will have tribulation. But take heart; I have overcome the world."

Note the contrasts of "in me" versus "in the world" and "peace" versus "tribulation." Peace in Christ is the believer's reality. Tribulation is the precursor to the triumphant kingdom of God that Jesus brings through his coming victory.

Acts 5:41: "Then they left the presence of the council, rejoicing that they were counted worthy to suffer dishonor for the name."

The apostles rejoiced in the God-given privilege of identifying with Christ and sharing in his sufferings.

Romans 5:3–5: "More than that, we rejoice in our sufferings, knowing that suffering produces endurance, and endurance produces character, and character produces hope, and hope does not put us to shame, because God's love has been poured into our hearts through the Holy Spirit who has been given to us."

The word translated *sufferings* means "pressing in" on a person because of being a Christ follower. Joy is possible even during trials as we keep our focus on what God has promised to accomplish in and through us. The endurance required is not a passive reception but an active participation in the process of building faith, character, hope, and communion.

Romans 8:16–18: "The Spirit himself bears witness with our spirit that we are children of God, and if children, then heirs—heirs of God and fellow heirs with Christ, provided we suffer with him in order that we may also be glorified with him. For I consider that the sufferings of this present time are not worth comparing with the glory that is to be revealed to us."

Our present sufferings for Christ prove that we are children of God and heirs of glory in eternity with God.

Romans 8:28, 35: "And we know that for those who love God all things work together for good, for those who are called according to his purpose. . . . Who shall separate us from the love

of Christ? Shall tribulation, or distress, or persecution, or famine, or nakedness, or danger, or sword?"

Paul's belief was grounded in knowledge of God as well as personal experience with these kinds of trials, and by God's grace and power Paul always emerged triumphant.

Romans 12:15: "Rejoice with those who rejoice, weep with those who weep."

Love of others is the supreme mark of a life pleasing to God. One of the greatest demonstrations of love is the sharing of a joy or sorrow with others, regardless of our own situation.

2 Corinthians 1:3–5: "Blessed be the God and Father of our Lord Jesus Christ, the Father of mercies and God of all comfort, who comforts us in all our affliction, so that we may be able to comfort those who are in any affliction, with the comfort with which we ourselves are comforted by God. For as we share abundantly in Christ's sufferings, so through Christ we share abundantly in comfort too."

True comfort is found in the security of God's sovereignty. Comfort here does not mean ease but courage and boldness to endure our trials. Recipients of this kind of comfort are to be agents of the same—coming alongside others to encourage them.

2 Corinthians 1: 8–9; 12:7–10:

For we do not want you to be ignorant, brothers, of the affliction we experienced in Asia. For we were so utterly burdened beyond our strength that we despaired of life itself. Indeed, we felt that we had received the sentence of death. But that was to make us rely not on ourselves but on God who raises the dead.

. . . So to keep me from becoming conceited because of the surpassing greatness of the revelations, a thorn was given me in the flesh, a messenger of Satan to harass

me, to keep me from becoming conceited. Three times I pleaded with the Lord about this, that it should leave me. But he said to me, "My grace is sufficient for you, for my power is made perfect in weakness." Therefore I will boast all the more gladly of my weaknesses, so that the power of Christ may rest upon me. For the sake of Christ, then, I am content with weaknesses, insults, hardships, persecutions, and calamities. For when I am weak, then I am strong.

Paul's thorn in the flesh may have been a physical malady that was always met by God's sufficient grace. Trials kept Paul humble—dependent on Christ and more receptive to his strength. Paul did not allow his weaknesses to be an excuse for passivity. Instead, he could boast in his weaknesses because his confidence was embedded in the God who uses earthly limitations as ordained opportunities for displaying divine power and strength.

Philippians 1:12–14: "I want you to know, brothers, that what has happened to me has really served to advance the gospel, so that it has become known throughout the whole imperial guard and to all the rest that my imprisonment is for Christ. And most of the brothers, having become confident in the Lord by my imprisonment, are much more bold to speak the word without fear."

Paul, in confinement under the Roman imperial guard, was given a captive audience. Paul saw his suffering as a platform from which to preach the gospel and embody it in action.

Philippians 3:8–10: "Indeed, I count everything as loss because of the surpassing worth of knowing Christ Jesus my Lord. For his sake I have suffered the loss of all things and count them as rubbish, in order that I may gain Christ and be found in him, not having a righteousness of my own that comes from the law, but that which comes through faith in Christ, the righteousness

from God that depends on faith—that I may know him and the power of his resurrection, and may share his sufferings, becoming like him in his death."

Paul had quite an impressive resumé, but he counted it all as a loss compared to knowing Christ, being found in him, and becoming like Jesus in his death. Jesus' power is most clearly experienced when believers endure the same kind of sufferings he endured, that of being a faithful witness for God's kingdom.

Philippians 4:13 "I can do all things through him who strengthens me."

Whether he was in poverty or plenty, the secret of Paul's ability to be content was found in his need and dependency on the all-sufficient Christ, who continually infused him with divine power.

Hebrews 4:16: "Let us then with confidence draw near to the throne of grace, that we may receive mercy and find grace to help in time of need."

This verse climaxes and concludes the writer's encouragement to approach God through Jesus as the High Priest. God's throne is one of authority and power and also where grace is found. Drawing near to God refers to our prayers to him, who graciously dispenses help from heaven to those who need forgiveness and strength.

Hebrews 12:1–7:

Therefore, since we are surrounded by so great a cloud of witnesses, let us also lay aside every weight, and sin which clings so closely, and let us run with endurance the race that is set before us, looking to Jesus, the founder and perfecter of our faith, who for the joy that was set before him endured the cross, despising the shame, and is seated at the right hand of the throne of God.

Consider him who endured from sinners such hostility against himself, so that you may not grow weary or

fainthearted. In your struggle against sin you have not yet resisted to the point of shedding your blood. And have you forgotten the exhortation that addresses you as sons?

> "My son, do not regard lightly the discipline of the Lord, nor be weary when reproved by him. For the Lord disciplines the one he loves, and chastises every son whom he receives."

It is for discipline that you have to endure. God is treating you as sons. For what son is there whom his father does not discipline?

The writer of Hebrews encountered those who wanted to give up. Persecution weighed heavily on the hearts of those suffering. He directed their attention to Jesus' suffering as an antidote for discouragement in their circumstances. He also reminded them that enduring the sorrow of discipline from their loving heavenly Father was necessary for their training in holiness—God's goal for all his children.

James 1:2–4 "Count it all joy, my brothers, when you meet trials of various kinds, for you know that the testing of your faith produces steadfastness. And let steadfastness have its full effect, that you may be perfect and complete, lacking in nothing."

Suffering is an inevitable part of life. The "various kinds" literally means "many-colored." And the term *trials* covers a variety of tests—inner temptation to sin, external circumstances, or persecution of faith. Suffering is an effective crucible of character and faith. Far from being crushed, the one who endures grows toward wholeness. The joy expressed here is not an emotion but a state of mind, the contentment found in an unshakable trust in God. Joy is not synonymous with happiness. Happiness is a temporary feeling when circumstances are to our liking. Joy is the proper response and utter satisfaction with God and his ways of testing our faith.

James 1:12: "Blessed is the man who remains steadfast under trial, for when he has stood the test he will receive the crown of life, which God has promised to those who love him."

For the Christian, the joy experienced from meeting trials and temptations in steadfast and godly ways is a taste of the heavenly joy that awaits believers. The "crown of life" awarded by God is life eternal. The crown is life itself; so, for believers, God will prove himself trustworthy and faithful to that promise.

1 Peter 1:6–7: "In this you rejoice, though now for a little while, if necessary, you have been grieved by various trials, so that the tested genuineness of your faith—more precious than gold that perishes though it is tested by fire—may be found to result in praise and glory and honor at the revelation of Jesus Christ."

The apostle Peter recognized the reality of grief in Christians and contrasted the present trials with the future glorious revelation of Jesus. These tests were brought on by oppressors who sought to cause believers to lose hope and leave the faith. Fixing their eyes on the coming hope brought great consolation to suffering believers. Peter's convictions came from the belief that God is in purposeful control.

1 Peter 4:19: "Therefore let those who suffer according to God's will entrust their souls to a faithful Creator while doing good."

Peter addressed the kind of suffering endured by believers for their faith in Christ. Whatever the consequences, we are to live entrusting ourselves to God. The truth that our God is the Creator, a word used only here in the whole of the New Testament, is the basis for believing he can be trusted. After all, if he is the Creator and giver of life, he is fully capable to care for every detail of life. His changelessness is grounds for trusting him. This trust shows up in our "doing good," even while suffering.

1 Peter 5:9: "Resist him, firm in your faith, knowing that the same kinds of suffering are being experienced by your brotherhood throughout the world."

Resisting the Devil was a common theme for the early church. Resistance means standing "firm in . . . faith," or, in other words, remaining firm in trusting God. Knowing that there is unity in suffering strengthens commitment. Christians do not suffer alone.

Food for Thought

The new year and decade began for the island nation of Haiti, the poorest nation in the Western Hemisphere, with a devastating 7.0 earthquake on January 12, 2010. Aftershocks continued to unnerve the living, while thousands of bodies remained trapped beneath the debris and wreckage of houses, stores, offices, and churches. Roads were difficult to maneuver as cars had to make their way around dead bodies, too numerous to be even temporarily housed. Families were torn apart. Children were left without parents, orphans left without housing facilities or food, and numerous family members suddenly gone, buried under tons of concrete, plaster, and wood. The death toll would come to over 200,000 in its capital and largest city, Port-au-Prince. Unimaginable suffering.

The response to Haiti's suffering was overwhelming and worldwide. And because we have all experienced pain, we resonated with the suffering in Haiti. We learn to respond to others' suffering particularly when human heartache hits our home, not just close to home.

The glass pane of life shatters when afflictions strike. Shards of what once was a beautiful thing lie scattered about. Pain is in the present reality and also in the lingering realization that things will never be the same. It is lonely there. We ask God why and for vindication. We wonder, What did I do wrong? Have I not prayed enough? Maybe I didn't have enough faith? These questions reveal a formulaic view of faith, that somehow if I do all the

right things God will surely keep me from pain. The goodness and love of God are often questioned in suffering. And his divine silence further buckles our knees in desperation. Making sense of gut-wrenching heartache challenges our understanding of God, as he will not be devalued by fitting into a formula.

The biblical character Job can be a faithful friend to us in times of suffering. He knew what loss of family and health and wealth felt like. He lost it all, and for no apparent reason. His friends tried to figure it out for him, arguing that some hidden or forgotten sin had caused his personal calamity. Finally God stepped in and began asking pointed questions of Job. You'll find them in chapters 38–41 in the book of Job. Each of God's matter-of-fact questions about the universe and kingdoms of the world proved Job's ignorance of how God rules his creation. Job became silent. God never answered Job's questions of why he was suffering, but Job learned more about the personal presence and sovereignty of God this way than had God answered his why question. Job then confessed while he was still in his suffering, "I know that you can do all things, and that no purpose of yours can be thwarted. . . . I have uttered what I did not understand, things too wonderful for me, which I did not know. . . . Therefore I despise myself, and repent in dust and ashes" (Job 42:2–3, 6). The character of God remains unchanged, regardless of human circumstances. That makes him worthy of our trust.

The shards of glass? God was present. He saw, heard, felt everything. When you started sweeping the pieces up, he was right there. He guided you to see the pieces that had flown beyond your blurred gaze. He gave you the very strength to maneuver the broom. He heard your cries and counted your tears (Psalm 56:8). God shares the sacred night of the soul with us.

The sacred night of the soul has no boundary of time. It can be as short as a literal night or as long as what seems a lifetime. Regardless, its memories refuse to be bound. What more clearly defines the sacred night is the state of the soul. When

the tides of tragedy drown out the sounds of hope, the nearness of God seems to recede. As the frail hope of a quick fix disappears, we learn that our true hope lies in knowing God's intimate presence in the sacred night. His suffering encompasses ours. We experience ourselves present with him in his divine sanctuary, drawing us ever nearer with his healing embrace. Love characterizes the sacred night of the soul because his presence is a grace bestowed. And at the moment we sense his confident trust in us, we can hear his affirming voice say, "Show them how it's done, beloved, when a righteous one who trusts in me suffers."

Some in Haiti know this. They have walked the path of suffering, yet they are certain of the goodness of God. The scenes are unforgettable: homeless Haitians living in temporary tents in the streets in desperate heartache, gathering to sing "How Great Thou Art." They sang in Creole. The nearby Americans started singing in American English. The French Canadians started singing in French. They were showing the world how it's done.

How To

Sometimes our suffering is a result of our own doing, sometimes of another's. The fear of revisiting the emotions associated with reopening the wound may have grown so deep that it has paralyzed us from moving forward toward wholeness. We have grown accustomed to the weight of this pain. As much as we long to be rid of this weight, the fear of the process outweighs any desire. God's desire is for a courageous heart, where he supplies the courage. He knows that a godly approach to pain and suffering can restore health to our souls.

Carve out time to spend in the presence of God for the purpose of bringing before him a time of suffering that continues to weigh on your heart. It may even be a present experience. Here are a few questions you can ask God as you listen for his response.

- Where were (are) you?
- What did (do) you hear?
- What did (do) you see?
- What do you want to say to me?
- Is there anyone you want me to forgive?
- Will you help me begin the process of forgiving?
- Will you remind me that I am yours?
- How do you want to show your strength in my weakness?

Allowing others to enter into our pain is another part of God's design. Consider his leading to avail yourself to grieve and to let your pain be known to a trusted friend.

There are some factors to remember for those who are in close community with one who suffers. Feelings of helplessness are common, but our discomfort can be mixed with a dose of pride in thinking that if we can give just the right Bible verse, pray just the right prayer, offer the perfect solution, then all will be fine once again. We fall into a similar pattern to that of Job's friends, wanting to correct Job instead of coming alongside him. We need "Don't fix me" grace. This is the Spirit-inspired grace to know the difference between caring and curing. It is grace that understands the difference between pushing a pragmatic fix and being present to feel and enter into another's pain, of allowing that pain to break our hearts without shouldering the pride-prone expectation to heal the wounded one. Consider simply the time to be still and quiet in the presence of another. May our simple presence mirror the committed presence of God.

Pitfalls

Untruths

Believing that suffering is a forbidden sign of weakness and therefore requires more control over circumstances only deepens personal shame and guilt. Avoidance, fear, detachment, and

aloneness are inevitable outcomes. Suffering is universal, and the failure to address its impact and effects robs human beings of the uniquely divine purposes found only in such circumstances.

Mundane Suffering

The slow grind of ordinary suffering, often submerged just under the surface of everyday life, dulls the senses to God and warps our theology, and from this place doubts begin to rise. But it is there, too, where the beauty of the presence of God lies, in the mundane suffering of the sacred night of the soul.

God's Stirring

Recognizing God's presence in these sacred nights brings light to the soul. We learn that fear is not the only option. Our cynical tendencies are reduced and strength begins to return. The truth of the nearness of God brings a glimmer of hope.

God also creates in us an unprecedented depth in living in community as it responds to suffering. Façades become unnecessary, and authentic communion with God and one another becomes the new normal.

Reflections from the Heart

- I would never have chosen to go through that, but I see now how much intimacy the Lord allowed me to have with him, as I would sit and cry in the palm of his hand. The comfort that I found in him was like nothing I had ever experienced before that time. *Kimberly B.*

- In suffering, I have exercised not only greater faith in myself, but also greater faith in God. I pray, read my Bible, and am more attentive and receptive to what God is saying during the period of suffering. I should be doing this all of the time, whether suffering or not, but that is not always the case. I need to become more reliant on God and not on myself. *Jason S.*

- An important discipline that goes less recognized is suffering and how the believer is to respond to it. Contemporary American culture would suggest that suffering is to be avoided. We are to do all that we can to avoid discomfort. But we read in the Bible that suffering is a legitimate part of the growth of a Christian. As gold is refined in the fire, so God refines us. My own experience has taught me that there are no times when God feels nearer than when I am suffering. Not only do I get a sense of how hopelessly helpless I am without him, but I can also feel his presence and love more than during any other type of experience. It has been during these times of suffering that I have grown the most in my relationship with God and learned the most about his character. It is easy to take God for granted during times of peace and pleasure, but I quickly learn to appreciate my relationship with him when I am suffering. *Matthew T.*

- Looking back in those difficult months of uncertainty and pleading with God, I am able to see how he was able to open wide my heart to make more room for dependency on him. I was [forced] to be honest with him, and I was so tired of being spiritually stagnant that I no longer became ashamed to present my greatest doubts and fears before the Lord. I can now see how God used this time to bring me closer to him. I have never experienced so much growth in such a short amount of time, and the joy that I have in serving him, being in his presence, and worshiping him for who he is, as so worth the struggle it took to get there. I am so thankful for the desolate place I was in before because I got to watch how God would lead me out. *Veronica B.*

- This past week, when I was reflecting on both my past and current sufferings, instead of feeling burdened by them, I embraced them. This is an attitude I have never adopted when approaching difficult things in my life, and I think

that is a positive step forward for me. Often, I get stuck in the trap of, "Hey, how are you?" "I'm good. How are you?" "I'm good." This is where a majority of my conversations in passing dwelled. When I realized it, my interactions felt so meaningless and hollow. Then I realized this is how I portray my sufferings, just passing them off and leaving them under the surface. Suffering should not be passed off as insignificant; there is a deeper meaning behind it that only God can determine. . . . Another thing that I realized was that in my sufferings, I turn away from God instead of toward him. This makes no sense to me, yet I continue this silly cycle in my daily life. . . . I simply throw myself a pity party and try to slowly get myself out of the mess I am in. This is the complete opposite response than I wish I had. *Rachel M.*

Fill in the Blank

Suffering breaks the seduction of _____ and allows me the hear God's invitation to/for _____.

Closing Thought

The sacred night of the soul offers us a God-ordained opportunity for deep intimacy with him. You can trust in his promised abiding presence because of who he is, and whether we feel it or not, who he is never changes.

Helpful Reads

John Hutchison, *Thinking Right When Things Go Wrong: Biblical Wisdom for Surviving Tough Times* (Grand Rapids: Kregel Publications, 2005).

Klaus Issler, *Wasting Time with God: A Christian Spirituality of Friendship with God* (Downers Grove: InterVarsity Press, 2001), chapter 7.

John Ortberg, *The Life You've Always Wanted: Spiritual Disciplines for Ordinary People* (Grand Rapids: Zondervan, 2004), chapter 13.

9
BIBLICAL HOSPITALITY: THIS STRANGER, MY FRIEND

Definition: The grateful response to God's extension of saving grace in indiscriminant acts of generosity and friendship toward strangers—fellow image bearers of God—while expecting nothing in return. Society's "unlovable" become the object of those whose hands, feet, voices, and presence embody Christ. Their hearts, like God's, beat for the last, least, and lost because of his desire that they be first, favored, and found.

Letting the Word Speak

Old Testament

Leviticus 19:33–34: "When a stranger sojourns with you in your land, you shall not do him wrong. You shall treat the stranger who sojourns with you as the native among you, and you shall love him as yourself, for you were strangers in the land of Egypt: I am the LORD your God." (See also Ezekiel 47:23 and Numbers 9:14.)

The Israelites knew what it was like to be strangers; they had been strangers in Egypt. In turn they were to consider the foreigners among them and treat them as one of their own. The extension of friendship crossed racial barriers, and this reflected God's heart.

Job 31:32: "The sojourner has not lodged in the street; I have opened my doors to the traveler."

Nearly four thousand years ago, Job insisted that, contrary to a friend's charge, he had not neglected those outside of his household. Job had been gracious to strangers, extending to them generous hospitality.

New Testament

Matthew 25:35: "For I was hungry and you gave me food, I was thirsty and you gave me drink, I was a stranger and you welcomed me."

In a parable of Jesus about the final judgment, we find that our eternal destiny is connected with how we care for the particularly needy in God's family. One indicator of true discipleship is biblical hospitality.

Luke 14:12–14: "He said also to the man who had invited him, 'When you give a dinner or a banquet, do not invite your friends or your brothers or your relatives or rich neighbors, lest they also invite you in return and you be repaid. But when you give a feast, invite the poor, the crippled, the lame, the blind, and you will be blessed, because they cannot repay you. For you will be repaid at the resurrection of the just.'"

The best hospitality is given, not exchanged. Jesus calls us to be especially mindful of those who cannot repay our kindnesses.

Romans 12:13: "Contribute to the needs of the saints and seek to show hospitality."

God commands hospitality to be extended, as it was a necessity for early Christians, most of whom could not afford hotels (lodging houses) when traveling. They were dependent on the provision of fellow believers. If we think these were always close friends, the Greek word used here for hospitality means "love of strangers."

1 Timothy 3:2: "Therefore an overseer must be above reproach, the husband of one wife, sober-minded, self-controlled, respectable, hospitable, able to teach."

As one of the qualifications for church leaders, hospitality would be the evidence of what they taught. Action-affirming words and word-affirming actions characterized these leaders who were to be models in their communities.

1 Timothy 5:9–10: "Let a widow be enrolled if she is not less than sixty years of age, having been the wife of one husband, and having a reputation for good works: if she has brought up children, has shown hospitality, has washed the feet of the saints, has cared for the afflicted, and has devoted herself to every good work."

The list of qualifications for receiving financial support from the church included the requirement that a widow be characterized as one who was hospitable, to have "lodged strangers."

Titus 1:7–8: "For an overseer, as God's steward, must be above reproach. He must not be arrogant or quick-tempered or a drunkard or violent or greedy for gain, but hospitable, a lover of good, self-controlled, upright, holy, and disciplined."

The first of the positive attributes of a godly leader is being hospitable. Here the Greek word *philoxenos*, "lover of strangers," is used for hospitality.

Hebrews 13:1–2: "Let brotherly love continue. Do not neglect to show hospitality to strangers, for thereby some have entertained angels unawares. Remember those who are in prison, as though in prison with them, and those who are mistreated, since you also are in the body."

Hospitality is commanded by God in order to engage with the world, and don't be surprised if you actually minister to strangers who are out of this world, literally.

1 Peter 4:9: "Show hospitality to one another without grumbling."

The early church regularly expressed its love for one another within the context of hospitality, as inns for travelers were expensive, potentially dangerous, and often unpleasant. This was accomplished by receiving others into your home, making them feel welcome, meeting their needs, and providing them with a place of fellowship and acceptance. All this, as Peter added, "without grumbling." Whiny hosts miss the hospitality mark.

Food for Thought

Cookies and punch come to mind at the mention of hospitality. Hospitality sign-up sheets enlist volunteers to greet visitors and ensure there is coffee ready to be served. Others think of having friends over and skillfully exercising their "Martha Stewart" flair for entertaining. As such, hospitality is often associated with the female gender, since women are usually the ones who plan, prepare, execute, and enjoy creating a welcoming atmosphere for gatherings, wherever they might be.

God's understanding of hospitality, though, offers a different perspective. The Greek word *philoxenos*, meaning "lover of strangers," combines the word for love or affection for people who are connected by kinship or faith (*phileo*) with the word for stranger (*xenos*). This word is translated *hospitable* in Titus 1:8 and 1 Peter 4:9; and *philoxenia*, "love of strangers," is translated *hospitality* in Romans 12:13 and Hebrews 13:2. The sense of the word includes an element of delight from this relationship. There is a mutual welcoming in this means of grace with an anticipation of witnessing God's role in it.

The word doesn't appear in the Old Testament, but its practice clearly does. Abraham and Sarah welcomed the three heavenly visitors (Genesis 18); the widow of Zarephath welcomed Elijah with what little she had (1 Kings 17); and God commanded his people to treat those without a home as one of their own, with

love (Leviticus 19:33–34). In the New Testament, hospitality is foundational in many of the events in Jesus' life and ministry as well as in the early Christian community. Christians were commended for entertaining strangers in their homes, and this was an expectation for church leaders.

This kind of biblical hospitality extended toward a stranger was a sacred duty throughout the Mediterranean world. It involved receiving, feeding, lodging, and protecting any traveler who might come to the door. The stranger became a guest and was treated with respect and honor. Water for dusty feet, a place to rest, and a sumptuous feast—and even feed for the animals—were provided. This act was meant to forge friendship ties unlike any other.

In our English dictionaries, *xenophilia* is an attraction to foreign peoples, cultures, or customs. More than a great word for Scrabble or Words with Friends, this should more typify Christian hospitality than the usual default, xenophobia.

In our contemporary times, Parker Palmer described hospitality as "inviting the stranger into our private space, whether that be the space of our home or the space of our personal awareness and concern. And when we do so, some important transformations occur. Our private space is suddenly enlarged; no longer tight and cramped and restricted, but open and expansive and free. And our space may also be illumined. . . . Hospitality to the stranger gives us a chance to see our own lives afresh, through different eyes."[1]

As such, the meaning of *hospitality* needs to be limited to the benevolence done to those outside our normal circles of friends. It will likely involve someone who doesn't look, dress, talk, or live like us because it is extended irrespective of race, class, ethnicity, financial standing, emotional, physical, or social status and does not require the other to "have it all together" in order to warrant attention.

A case in point is the friendship between Mickey and Greg. Mickey is one of my New Testament colleagues. He is a large-

framed former college football player. Think John Calvin in a John Madden body. Mickey serves his church in the college ministry. That is where he met Greg. Greg is a twenty-year-old tough guy who has had a difficult life. At a time in life when many people are finishing their education and looking forward to being in the business world, Greg is combating the effects of years of drug and alcohol addiction. His gangster hat and clothes don't tell the story of being kicked out of his home when he was eight or having lived in a boys' home until he was eighteen. His speech doesn't tell of him making money as a pimp, getting into trouble with the law, being shot at in an alley and hearing two of the four bullets whiz by his ear. His nearly four hundred pounds of rough, cocky, authority-hating "rebellion with skill" mask an even larger void of genuine care and sincere love.

It wasn't Mickey's ability to argue sound theological tenets of Christianity or key themes of Johannine literature (impressive to any number of us) or his ability to chest bump and wrestle with the best of them that resonated with Greg, but the fact that Mickey had grown up without a dad. Greg's dad died when he was eleven, and he missed him desperately. Greg couldn't believe it when Mickey invited him to join his family for dinner and that he was allowed to eat at the same table with Mickey's wife, Laura, and their two young sons. Upon seeing the family dynamics in Mickey's home, Greg once remarked, "That was the most amazing thing I've ever seen."

I can only imagine what God saw: a stranger being touched by the friendship of God. The power of the gospel can make people who once were strangers into wonderful friends.

How To

Biblical hospitality isn't a "been there, done that" deal. This would just amount to something done in our own power and for our own purposes. Be sure to ponder the truth that God first extended his divine friendship to us when we were sinners—unlovable, unworthy, and objects of his wrath. But because of Christ, the Father invited us in and things are different. We are different. Be alert and sensitive and then obedient to God's Spirit so that his prompting to extend friendship to a stranger will not be ignored or suppressed. God will lead you to the "who, what, where, and when"; you've just learned the why.

Pitfalls

Insecurity

Loving God is not easy for us to translate into love for strangers. What will other people think when I talk to someone who is disheveled and homeless, an "illegal alien," or someone who has more or less melanin in his or her skin cells than I? As we grow less dependent on what other people think and more concerned with what God thinks, he develops in us a diminished preoccupation with our own image and a greater sense of being bearers of his image.

Failure to Remember

God always initiates. He has extended his friendship to a world of strangers, and he did so intimately through Jesus Christ. Reading the Gospel records of Jesus' life on earth, we see the God-man being a recipient of hospitality as an itinerant teacher and rabbi. Ultimately, he brings the gospel message of forgiveness that through his life, death, and resurrection we now have a friendship with God. We sometimes fail to remember that the friendship we extend to others is because of the divine friendship we have and will enjoy forever. We graciously befriend others because God so graciously befriended us.

God's Stirring

As the sphere of those who call you "friend" enlarges, your soul is impacted. Rather than feeling robbed of time and energy, you can begin to take humble pleasure in a greater sense of well-being, a

sense that the God of the universe had a part in this encounter. Perhaps that stranger is just a friend you have not yet met.

Reflections from the Heart

- Her name was Keirston, and she seemed to be in need of a friend to talk with. By talking with her, I realized that she lives apart from God, and when we spoke, the topic of God came up, so I shared what God has done in my life and why I now am devoted to him. . . . She has a daughter, and we talked about what a child needs to be healthy, and at the end of the conversation it felt like she wanted to keep listening about good and positive qualities for better living. . . . I feel that this hospitality opportunity has opened the door for me to get to know someone who probably doesn't have a Christian friend in their life and may open the door for them to reach to God one day, who knows? *David L.*

- God revealed to me how I have, as Peter puts it, grumbled while showing hospitality to others. My heart didn't align with Jesus', though my outward actions appeared to have. This week I had a really awesome opportunity to exercise hospitality by extending friendship and time to someone whom I wouldn't necessarily hang out with. Instead of just the usual, "Hello, how are you?" I took time to really talk and listen to this person. I sort of think of it as welcoming them into my heart (rather than home) by really listening and caring about them. Too many times in the past I remember treating people as if they were merely a roadblock in my day, as if they were getting in my way of my true objectives for the day. That doesn't sound like Christ at all. I want to see people as God sees them and treat them like they are just as important as myself and my own needs. Getting a more biblical understanding of hospitality has helped me see more clearly what God's own heart looks like in this means of grace. *Eric A.*

- I am hesitant to extend myself, because I am afraid I have nothing to extend. I am "waiting" for a time when I will be in a better position to be hospitable.

  This is often how every period of my life has been so far.

  When I'm a teenager, then I will be more ready to make an impact!

  When I'm in college, then I will be responsible.

  When I have my own place, then I can truly be selfless toward people and live for Christ!

  When I'm married, then I will have things to share, abilities to mentor, and faculties to influence people.

  This is a tactic of the Evil One to keep me from ever making an impact. I always have an excuse, always. The desire and the dreams to be hospitable are not enough! And it doesn't help that I have had a limited view of hospitality up till this point. *Andrea M.*

- A misconception of hospitality is that it only applies for practice to those who have some kind of leadership within the church, or have been given the spiritual gift of hospitality. This is far from the truth, for all within the body are called to be hospitable. We don't offer this to those we just know, but to the individuals who for the first time have crossed our eyes. Those who for the first time have crossed our eyes, whether Christians or not, should be served the best steak, eggs, donuts, and peanut butter and jelly sandwiches, for we are called not to show favoritism in anyway. If we are able to do this well, then our actions will show the character of God. *Juan F.*

- Spending time with others has been a challenge this semester because of the season I am in right now, but through this means of grace, God showed me that no matter how "busy" I may be, extending love and friendship to others at all times is what will distinguish me as his follower. *Rosio M.*

- I started doing that [hospitality] by keeping my promises to those I would normally flake out on. I have a tendency to ditch people or text people I made plans with at the last minute, just because I thought that they weren't "important" enough. I was about to text [a friend] and said, "No. I must show hospitality." So I went to the café and met up with her, and wow. I am so glad I did not cancel on her. It turns out that she's been hurting a lot lately by realizing who her true friends are, and she was telling me how she feels as though so many people neglect her and how many people cancel things on her because they're just too busy.

  This broke my heart. I've always been that person. I was always too busy for certain people because I thought I was more important and they weren't important enough. I was the neglecter, and right in front of me, I was now having dinner with the girl who has always been the neglectee. And I got to see a glimpse of the pain I had caused people whenever I neglected them because I was too careless and too self-absorbed. We had an amazing talk afterward, and we plan to hang out much more often now. And, no, I will not neglect her, but I am going to stand beside her because she is my sister in Christ. And if you can't count on family, who can you count on? *Caroline N.*

Fill in the Blank

Biblical hospitality breaks the seduction of _____ and allows me to hear God's invitation to/for _____.

Closing Thought

The heart of God is clearly revealed through biblical hospitality as those who call themselves Christians extend friendship across racial, ethnic, status, and class barriers so others can experience a glimpse of God's abundance in his kingdom. God has extended his friendship to strangers of the most deprived sort; how can we do any less?

Helpful Reads

Klaus Issler, *Wasting Time with God: A Christian Spirituality of Friendship with God* (Downers Grove: InterVarsity Press, 2001), chapter 2.

John Koenig, *New Testament Hospitality: Partnership with Strangers as Promise and Mission* (Eugene, OR: Wipf and Stock Publishers, 1985).

10
BIBLICAL THANKSGIVING:
THE HEADS-UP ON *HESED*

Definition: The humble and responsive posture of the heart that expresses gratitude regardless of circumstances because it simply focuses on who God is and what he does. It starts with the internal recognition of our core needs and the acknowledgment of an all-knowing God and his loving-kindness—*hesed*. This is followed by an external expression of dependence on and adoration of God. We extend this thankfulness to those among us who are conscious or unconscious conduits of God's *hesed*. It is not found in a moment, a holiday, or a meal, but in a way of thinking and living wisely.

Letting the Word Speak

Old Testament

Psalm 50:14: "Offer to God a sacrifice of thanksgiving, and perform your vows to the Most High."

The point of thank offerings was that such sacrifices acknowledged the offerer's absolute dependence on Yahweh's grace and mercy. God received many different sacrifices, but what he really desired was the praise and thanksgiving of his people. God wants the person behind the sacrifice.

Psalm 107:8–9: "Let them thank the LORD for his steadfast love, for his wondrous works to the children of man! For he satisfies the longing soul, and the hungry soul he fills with good things."

The mighty acts of God, as promises fulfilled by him, formed the history of Israel that was the basis for their relationship. When the past is remembered in thanksgiving, trust for God to act again is developed and nurtured. The proper response is to thank the Lord for his unfailing love.

Psalm 136:1–3 "Give thanks to the LORD, for he is good, for his steadfast love endures forever. Give thanks to the God of gods, for his steadfast love endures forever. Give thanks to the Lord of lords, for his steadfast love endures forever."

In Jewish tradition Psalm 136 has been called the Great Psalm of Praise. The phrase "Give thanks" is repeated in the opening three verses of this psalm. "For his steadfast love endures forever" forms the second line of each of the psalm's twenty-six verses. Its repetition served as a reminder of God's unwavering love throughout Israel's history and served to deepen the truth of God's loving character in the hearts of all who sang or listened to this hymn.

New Testament

Matthew 14:19: "Then he ordered the crowds to sit down on the grass, and taking the five loaves and the two fish, he looked up to heaven and said a blessing. Then he broke the loaves and gave them to the disciples, and the disciples gave them to the crowds." (See also Luke 9:16.)

Looking up to heaven reflects a common posture for prayer. Jesus blessed God for the bread and for his imminent miraculous provision for the crowd of over five thousand hungry people. From a seemingly endless supply of bun-sized loaves and dried or pickled fish, the disciples distributed the food and all present were

satisfied. Jesus performed this miracle out of compassion for the hungry people. He demonstrated kingdom authority while showing his gratitude to and dependence on his Father.

Luke 17:11–19:

> On the way to Jerusalem he was passing along between Samaria and Galilee. And as he entered a village, he was met by ten lepers, who stood at a distance and lifted up their voices, saying, "Jesus, Master, have mercy on us." When he saw them he said to them, "Go and show yourselves to the priests." And as they went they were cleansed. Then one of them, when he saw that he was healed, turned back, praising God with a loud voice; and he fell on his face at Jesus' feet, giving him thanks. Now he was a Samaritan. Then Jesus answered, "Were not ten cleansed? Where are the nine? Was no one found to return and give praise to God except this foreigner?" And he said to him, "Rise and go your way; your faith has made you well."

All ten lepers recognized Jesus' authority and called out to him for mercy. Though all received his mercy, compassion, and complete healing, only one returned to thank him—a Samaritan. We might have expected all the lepers to respond in gratitude, but only one did. A despised half-breed and social outcast whose leprosy deemed him socially and ceremonially unclean became the model for responding to grace. A worshipful response to grace can come from the most unexpected sources.

Romans 1:20–21: "For his invisible attributes, namely, his eternal power and divine nature, have been clearly perceived, ever since the creation of the world, in the things that have been made. So they are without excuse. For although they knew God, they did not honor him as God or give thanks to him, but they became futile in their thinking, and their foolish hearts were darkened."

Creation testifies of God's person and power. John Calvin saw the world as a theater where the glory of God is always on display. We may choose to reject, suppress, or even distort that evidence, creating our own reality or version of it; but that doesn't make it any less true. Deep down, all human beings know there is God and are therefore accountable to him. Refraining from worship or giving thanks is equivalent to willful rebellion and rejection of God's lordship. Ingratitude is a distinguishing mark of nonbelievers, a sign of a grandiose self-image. The proper response is to praise and thank God. Thankfulness characterizes the people of God

Romans 6:17: "But thanks be to God, that you who were once slaves of sin have become obedient from the heart to the standard of teaching to which you were committed."

Paul thanked God for the love and faith the Roman Christians experienced. God rescued them from sin's dominion, where they were slaves of sin but became obedient to the gospel. He thanked God for their obedience, for it is God who causes obedience. The transformation that began in their hearts at conversion continued toward wholeness.

1 Corinthians 4:7 "For who sees anything different in you? What do you have that you did not receive? If then you received it, why do you boast as if you did not receive it?"

There is no basis for inflated egos. Understanding that divine grace has distributed to us every blessing we have calls forth our gratitude and humility and negates our pride. For the Corinthians to be puffed up against each other effectively denied that God is the one who had given them all things. "What do you have that you did not receive?" Pondering this simple question can have a powerful impact on your heart's humility and thanksgiving quotient.

1 Corinthians 15:57: "But thanks be to God, who gives us the victory through our Lord Jesus Christ."

Victory would be a familiar word to the Corinthians, as victory songs from the Isthmian Games of Corinth would have echoed in their minds. Paul's focus for his thanksgiving was God, whose victory over death—won through Christ and his resurrection—is now shared with all believers.

Ephesians 1:16: "I do not cease to give thanks for you, remembering you in my prayers."

As was typical of Paul's letters, he gave thanks to God for Christ's work evident in his readers. He was so focused on God's goodness being manifested through the love and faith of the Ephesian church that he could not stop thanking and praising God. Negative things frequently motivate people to pray, but the good things more often motivated Paul. He responded by thanking God.

Ephesians 5:3–5: "But sexual immorality and all impurity or covetousness must not even be named among you, as is proper among saints. Let there be no filthiness nor foolish talk nor crude joking, which are out of place, but instead let there be thanksgiving. For you may be sure of this, that everyone who is sexually immoral or impure, or who is covetous (that is, an idolater), has no inheritance in the kingdom of Christ and God."

Thanksgiving was to replace the six vices at the heart and verbiage of Christian speech. The antidote to self-centered greed is the intentional mindfulness of God's generosity. A few verses later (verse 20), Paul asserted thanksgiving as a mark of being filled with God's Spirit. Biblical thanksgiving allows us to focus on the gracious blessings of God as opposed to coveting what others have. Gratitude is transformational.

Philippians 4:5–6: "The Lord is at hand; do not be anxious about anything, but in everything by prayer and supplication with thanksgiving let your requests be made known to God. And the peace of God, which surpasses all understanding, will guard your hearts and your minds in Christ Jesus."

The Philippian church was threatened by quarrels within and enemies without, fueling anxiety and discontent. Paul understood prayer and requests with thanksgiving to be the antidote to potential chaos. Submitting concerns and needs to God with an attitude of thankfulness for who he is and what he has already given yields unshakable trust, contentment, and peace.

Colossians 3:15–17: "And let the peace of Christ rule in your hearts, to which indeed you were called in one body. And be thankful. Let the word of Christ dwell in you richly, teaching and admonishing one another in all wisdom, singing psalms and hymns and spiritual songs, with thankfulness in your hearts to God. And whatever you do, in word or deed, do everything in the name of the Lord Jesus, giving thanks to God the Father through him."

Three times in three verses some form of the word *thanks* is used: being thankful, singing thanks to God, and expressing thanks to God. When infused with thanksgiving, mundane activities become acts of worship. Gratitude is a distinctive feature that characterizes the Christian life.

1 Thessalonians 5:16–18: "Rejoice always, pray without ceasing, give thanks in all circumstances; for this is the will of God in Christ Jesus for you."

Praying without ceasing sounds impossible, but what is described here is prayerfulness as a lifestyle, where prayer doesn't end with an amen but instead lingers. Circumstances do not dictate whether or not gratitude is expressed. C. S. Lewis penned, "We ought to give thanks for all fortune: if it is "good," because it is good, if "bad" because it works in us patience, humility and the contempt of this world and the hope of our eternal country."[1]

The sanctifying work of the Spirit finds expression in rejoicing, praying, and giving thanks. This is God's will: Be joyful, talk often with God, and give thanks. Thanksgiving is deeply rooted

in Paul's theology; he believed that God is at work in all circumstances on behalf of his people.

1 Timothy 2:1: "First of all, then, I urge that supplications, prayers, intercessions, and thanksgivings be made for all people."

Regardless of things that keep people apart, prayer is to be offered for all people. This would have been extraordinary in the age of the Roman emperors and local authorities known to be ruthless. No one was to be excluded when it came to a believer's prayer.

2 Timothy 3:2: "For people will be lovers of self, lovers of money, proud, arrogant, abusive, disobedient to their parents, ungrateful, unholy."

Paul described the false teachers in the self-centeredness of their actions and attitudes. Their moral decline paved the way for their wrong teaching. Ingratitude is an indication of their arrogance.

Revelation 11:16–17: "And the twenty-four elders who sit on their thrones before God fell on their faces and worshiped God, saying,

> 'We give thanks to you, Lord God Almighty,
>> who is and who was,
> for you have taken your great power
>> and begun to reign.'"

In this vision God has come to take his place as King of the universe. There is praise here for him being recognized as King and exercising his power as God and ruler forever. Heaven will be filled with the voices of angelic creatures and of the redeemed giving thanks to God. Hymns of praise and thanksgiving are a common feature in Revelation's descriptions of heavenly worship. Our thanksgiving will continue in heaven and will continue for all eternity. In the meantime, we are in the dress rehearsal.

Food for Thought

Being grateful affects our well-being. Psychologists Robert Emmons and Michael McCullough are foremost researchers exploring the nature, causes, and consequences of gratitude. Their scientific research has and continues to show that our lives are positively impacted when attention is given to the things for which we are thankful. Physiologically, it is good to give thanks.[2]

In our contemporary times, giving thanks assumes recognition for some act of generosity received that could also be reciprocated. But in hierarchical societies there was a large chasm between the status of the giver and receiver. As the Creator of the universe is the giver, the receiver has no adequate way to reciprocate. The only proper response is the humble act of thanksgiving and praise for who he is and what he has done, admitting our total dependency on him.

Sixty-two times in the New Testament different forms of the Greek word *eucharistia* (related to the word *Eucharist*) are used to mean thanksgiving. Three-fourths of those occurrences are found in Paul's letters. In fact, Paul mentioned thanksgiving more frequently per page than any other Greek author, pagan or Christian. When placed in the introductory portion of a letter, he used this literary device to set the tone for the rest of his letter; it is always a response to God's saving activity in creation and redemption.

When Paul mentioned thanksgiving elsewhere, it was reserved for God, for his past acts of kindness and his future acts that affirm the supremacy of God as Creator and powerful orchestrator of his mighty acts. According to Paul it is the duty of all humankind to acknowledge God as Creator and give thanks to him.

Believers see God as the Creator, the provider of salvation, and the giver of every good and perfect gift. Paul's primary focus for thanksgiving was God, not his gifts. It is based on the gift of salvation through the death and resurrection of Christ, the redemptive power of God that overcame sin and the power of death. In the New Testament, the object of thanksgiving is the love of God expressed in the redemptive work of Christ. The apostle Paul thanked God for that gift of grace (1 Corinthians 1:4; 2 Corinthians 9:15). For Paul, a simple thank-you was insufficient; only worship and submission were appropriate.

A contemporary Greek scholar commented that Paul understood grace not simply as divine favor but also within the same semantic domain as the Hebrew term *hesed*, an Old Testament term usually translated "mercy" or "grace" in the New Testament.[3] What is striking about *hesed* is its radical, out-of-the-box, ethnic- and culture-transcending type of kindness.

I told a colleague of mine that the more I study *hesed*, the stronger the impression God makes on my soul. He told me to look at Psalm 33:5. As soon as I got back to my desk, this is what I read: "He loves righteousness and justice; the earth is full of the steadfast love of the LORD."

The earth is filled with God's *hesed*. It can be found in creation, in the gift of a treasured friendship, in a prayer or memorized verse, in a word divinely dropped for our hearing. But we miss so much of it. Here is just another reminder of the necessity to engage with God in this means of grace in order to grow more attentive and familiar with his radical kindnesses—his *hesed*.

Grace is the grounds for thanksgiving. This connection between grace and thanksgiving again points to the connection between thanksgiving and the mighty acts of God. In remembering these mighty acts, we are called to remember God and his Son through whom salvation history reaches its climax. And as a loving Father, God delights in giving good gifts to his children.

Biblical thanksgiving is expressed by the way Christ's followers live out their lives. Gratitude is an action. Our oral expressions of gratitude are shallow substitutes because to live a life worthy of the Lord is to live with a constant awareness of God's grace, his *hesed*. It is good to give thanks. It is good to live thankfully.

How To

Thanksgiving starts with a time of being still before God because our pace of life is not conducive to growing alert to recognizing God's *hesed* in our lives. But once we do, our souls are more adept at catch sightings of God's ubiquitous *hesed*. Our ability to be expectantly watchful is proportional to noticing more of God's radical mercy and grace. This type of watchfulness turns into thanksgiving from deep in our spirits.

Mary's Magnificat (Luke 1:46–55) follows the pattern of a psalm of thanksgiving, which first thanks God and then explains why the psalmist is thankful. Try writing your own Magnificat— your prayer or song of thanks to God, *magnifying* him for all he has done for you and for others.

Or take advantage of the *hesed* calendar at the end of this chapter. Carve out a reflective moment at the end of each day, and record any *hesed* sightings. In following the pattern of Psalm 136, pray, "For his steadfast love endures forever" after each entry. Prayerfully begin.

"Happiness experts" encourage people to jot down things they are grateful for. For deep-rooted, lifelong joy, however, offer your thanks to a caring, all-knowing, compassionate Father for who he is and whose mighty acts have culminated in his powerful gift of salvation and a certain hope for the future. Gratefulness cultivated for these grander themes extols God and will incorporate the smaller blessings; gratefulness limited only to smaller themes will miss out on the magnificent, greater God, who is then perceived as simply existing for our own purposes.

Pitfalls

Disillusionment

With the current events that appear on a telecast, in an online newspaper, or even as part of our daily conversations, it is easy to become skeptical about the state of our world. The inundation of

the ugliness, cruelty, and evil that surrounds us can mask recognition of the movements of God. What becomes our "normal" dulls our spiritual acuity, eclipsing the divine impressions on our spirits. Thanksgiving sharpens our spirits to God's blessings that surround us.

Entitlement

Our thanksgiving can be short lived or nonexistent when we feel a sense of entitlement. Underlying thankfulness is self-denial. Why give thanks for something I deserved in the first place? Pride in self-sufficiency is a major roadblock to an intimate life with God. Recalibrating ourselves by considering what we have been given by our heavenly Father moves our focus toward humble gratitude. What do we have that has not been given to us?

Displaced Thanks

Richard Greenham, an English Puritan, once penned, "Many are fervent in asking, but cold in giving thanks."[4] Take the opportunity to evaluate your relationship with God in light of your prayers. How much time and attention are given to the asking of things compared to the grateful receiving of more than had been asked for? Could it be that, like the nine ungrateful cleansed lepers, we are more enamored with the gift than the giver?

God's Stirring

Where the familiar acronym of A-C-T-S for prayer is used, there will be a greater understanding of the thanksgiving that follows confession. Thanksgiving becomes aligned with the gratefulness that accompanies receiving forgiveness for confessed sin. It is no longer the sudden shift from the act of confessing to a list of things we are grateful for, but rather a continuation of the flow that started with our adoration of God, to our recognition of our missing the mark, and then to the deep gratitude to God for his gracious and powerful acts in redemption and forgiveness.

As a lifestyle of acknowledging God's *hesed* helps to avoid the

temptation to align with the world's propensity to accumulate, it also leads to heart-inspired thanksgiving. We are not limited in means to express gratitude to God. It can be expressed through words and oral testimony, through song, with prayer, through service to others, out in the public, surrounded by a body of believers, privately at home, or even on a Facebook status. The transformation God accomplishes in us by way of our humbly recognizing and expressing thanks impacts our ability to reflect and extend his *hesed* to others. Uninhibited by the deluded self that tries to convince us that we do not need help, there is greater freedom and likelihood to express thankfulness.

Reflections from the Heart

- Practicing biblical thanksgiving was amazing. It gave me a new attitude and perspective on what is really important in life. This sounds so cliché, but I take for granted so many things in my life—I feel like the practice of biblical thanksgiving helps me to have a more grateful and gracious heart. I have felt more gracious and compassionate toward others after practicing this means of grace. *Teddi H.*

- Every morning this week, I woke up and just expressed thankfulness to God. And man, was it powerful. I found that the more I did this, the more throughout the day I was reminded to be thankful. It was contagious to my own self. The more I thanked God, the more of a thankful person I became. I learned that so much sin in our lives is really a result of ingratitude to God. Thankfulness really helps me escape micro thinking too, and it opens my eyes to the bigger picture of a God who is working universally to make all things new. I also noticed how much more "loose" I was with my own possessions and self-belongings. I was more ready to give and sacrifice because everything I had was a gift from God and not my own. *Zack A.*

- As I remember God and the blessings he has given me and give thanks to him, I become more aware of how much my life is blessed by him. I am able to put into perspective how my life is on my own strength as opposed to how my life is in Christ. Romans 1:20–21 has also been brought to mind multiple times since I read it. I have personally found that if I am not purposefully thankful for all the blessings I've been given, I tend to forget who I am in Christ, which leads to the "darkening" of my heart. I have also found that thanksgiving is a crucial part of remaining in Christ. Part of thanksgiving is remembrance, and if thanksgiving does not remain a part of our daily life, we will forget who we are in Christ. *Chris B.*

- I feel sometimes when I pray I go directly into asking God for what I want. I hardly ever thank him for everything he's already answered in my own life. Thanking God for his goodness, his mercy, and his blessings was great for me. I felt empowered and blessed myself. I also think that practicing biblical thanksgiving is kind of humbling. It showed me how much I cannot do by myself. It's only by God's enabling and mercy that I can do all things. This helped me a lot with humility, something that I struggle quite a bit with. Also, as mentioned earlier, thanking God was just a great form of praise for everything he is and has done. *Ben C.*

- There is nothing that makes me happier than thanking God for everything I have. When I do this, it makes me realize how much I have that I just don't deserve and makes me wonder how I could ever be discontent with life. It really just puts things in perspective for me when I think about where everything really comes from.. . . I see what happens to people when they do not exercise this means, and they are stuck in a state of mind where nothing is ever enough. They are always wanting more. Whenever I think about all I have been given and thank God for it, I just can't help but think the opposite

of these people and believe that I have been given too much. *Skyler C.*

- When I thank God simply for the things that make me feel good, then I learn to only be thankful when things are going well for me. When I thank God simply for who he is and the power and authority he has, then I learn to orient myself, my mood, and my thankfulness around something that doesn't change. My circumstances are constantly changing. God never changes. So if my thankfulness to God is dependent upon my circumstances, it's going to be changing all the time. However, if my gratitude is rooted in the unchanging perfection and power of God, it will be consistent and true. *Ariella B.*

- I had been in the habit of thanking God only on holidays or for the "big" things. However, this brief study revealed that biblical thanksgiving is an ongoing process that I should be practicing every minute of every day. In addition, my exercise of biblical thanksgiving before eating meals as well as learning to complain less frequently enabled me to recognize and appreciate God's providence in the small issues of life and revealed how much I depend on him for my daily sustenance. All in all, the practice of biblical thanksgiving allowed me to see just how unworthy I am of the amazing blessings that God has bestowed on me as well as helped me to trust God's wise and loving judgment in providing future blessings to be thankful for. *Sam S.*

Fill in the Blank

Biblical thanksgiving breaks the seduction of _____ and allows me to hear God's invitation to/for _____.

Closing Thought

God desires the ineffable to happen—when he makes a deep

impression on all we are that *he is God* and that he is fully present. And all we can do in response to his *hesed* is fall to our physical and spiritual knees in humble gratitude.

Helpful Reads

W. Bingham Hunter, *The God Who Hears* (Downers Grove: InterVarsity Press, 1986), chapter 8.

David Pao, *Thanksgiving: An Investigation of a Pauline Theme* (Downers Grove: InterVarsity Press, 2002).

Hesed Calendar

1	2	3	4	5	6	7
8	9	10	11	12	13	14
15	16	17	18	19	20	21
22	23	24	25	26	27	28
29	30	31				

11
SERVICE:
DONNING THE TOWEL

Definition: Born out of response to God's goodness and kindness, it is the lifestyle expression that tangibly reflects this goodness and kindness to others and to God. The depth, extent, and motivation for service, with its diminished need for recognition, are features that serve as evidence that God is the object of our service, his Son the model, and his Spirit the enabler.

Letting the Word Speak

Old Testament

Proverbs 14:35: "A servant who deals wisely has the king's favor, but his wrath falls on one who acts shamefully."

Those who pursue and live out wisdom, godly insight, and character in the simple and complex issues of life find favor in the eyes of others and God.

Proverbs 17:2: "A servant who deals wisely will rule over a son who acts shamefully and will share the inheritance as one of the brothers."

Though it is unlikely that a servant would receive an inheritance, the polar extremes serve to warn those who would shrink back from their responsibilities. Wisdom has advantages over birthright.

New Testament

Matthew 6:24: "No one can serve two masters, for either he will hate the one and love the other, or he will be devoted to the one and despise the other. You cannot serve God and money."

Jesus taught about having two treasures (6:19–21), two eyes (6:22–23), and here two masters. As a slave is the sole property of one master, Jesus taught that a true disciple can give exclusive, wholehearted service to only one master. Heavenly values will contrast with earthly ones: one produces treasures in heaven; the other produces treasures on earth. If God is our Master, anything else that detracts from our serving him with all our heart, soul, mind, and strength is a rival god.

Matthew 20:1–16:

> For the kingdom of heaven is like a master of a house who went out early in the morning to hire laborers for his vineyard. After agreeing with the laborers for a denarius a day, he sent them into his vineyard. And going out about the third hour he saw others standing idle in the marketplace, and to them he said, "You go into the vineyard too, and whatever is right I will give you." So they went. Going out again about the sixth hour and the ninth hour, he did the same. And about the eleventh hour he went out and found others standing. And he said to them, "Why do you stand here idle all day?" They said to him, "Because no one has hired us." He said to them, "You go into the vineyard too." And when evening came, the owner of the vineyard said to his foreman, "Call the laborers and pay them their wages, beginning with the last, up to the first." And when those hired about the eleventh hour came, each of them received a denarius. Now when those hired first came, they thought they would receive more, but

each of them also received a denarius. And on receiving it they grumbled at the master of the house, saying, "These last worked only one hour, and you have made them equal to us who have borne the burden of the day and the scorching heat." But he replied to one of them, "Friend, I am doing you no wrong. Did you not agree with me for a denarius? Take what belongs to you and go. I choose to give to this last worker as I give to you. Am I not allowed to do what I choose with what belongs to me? Or do you begrudge my generosity?" So the last will be first, and the first last.

If our service is motivated by the thought that somehow God rewards our diligence, sacrifice, and commitment to service, this leads to our expecting a reward, earning favor, comparing with others, and judging others' service. But if service is in humble response to God's positioning us in his kingdom in the first place, then others' service will be celebrated, and grumbling will find no place in our own acts of service.

Matthew 23:8–12: "But you are not to be called rabbi, for you have one teacher, and you are all brothers. And call no man your father on earth, for you have one Father, who is in heaven. Neither be called instructors, for you have one instructor, the Christ. The greatest among you shall be your servant. Whoever exalts himself will be humbled, and whoever humbles himself will be exalted."

The Pharisees adopted their world's model of leadership that promoted personal power, authority, and pride in their leaders by using these titles. Jesus addressed the legalistic burdens (23:1–4), the public displays of religiosity (23:5–7), and these titles of honor. The disciples' earlier lack of understanding about how leadership would function in God's kingdom prompted Jesus to teach about leaders as servants of those around them.

Matthew 25:31–46

When the Son of Man comes in his glory, and all the angels with him, then he will sit on his glorious throne. Before him will be gathered all the nations, and he will separate people one from another as a shepherd separates the sheep from the goats. And he will place the sheep on his right, but the goats on the left. Then the King will say to those on his right, "Come, you who are blessed by my Father, inherit the kingdom prepared for you from the foundation of the world. For I was hungry and you gave me food, I was thirsty and you gave me drink, I was a stranger and you welcomed me, I was naked and you clothed me, I was sick and you visited me, I was in prison and you came to me." Then the righteous will answer him, saying, "Lord, when did we see you hungry and feed you, or thirsty and give you drink? And when did we see you a stranger and welcome you, or naked and clothe you? And when did we see you sick or in prison and visit you?" And the King will answer them, "Truly, I say to you, as you did it to one of the least of these my brothers, you did it to me."

Then he will say to those on his left, "Depart from me, you cursed, into the eternal fire prepared for the devil and his angels. For I was hungry and you gave me no food, I was thirsty and you gave me no drink, I was a stranger and you did not welcome me, naked and you did not clothe me, sick and in prison and you did not visit me." Then they also will answer, saying, "Lord, when did we see you hungry or thirsty or a stranger or naked or sick or in prison, and did not minister to you?" Then he will answer them, saying, "Truly, I say to you, as you did not do it to one of the least of these, you did not do it to me." And these will go away into eternal punishment, but the righteous into eternal life.

This is the final scene in the Olivet Discourse and is found only in Matthew. Jesus told his disciples of the events that would accompany his return as the Son of Man and then taught them about watching, waiting, and being prepared. He gave promises of reward and warnings of judgment that would accompany his coming. As Christ followers await his second coming, their lives are to be characterized by service to "the least of these," as though they are serving Christ. Citizens of God's kingdom are to extend compassion in tangible ways to the hungry, to the thirsty, to strangers, and to those in need or in prison. By virtue of the King's compassionate nature, compassion is extended to all people.

Mark 9:35: "And he sat down and called the twelve. And he said to them, 'If anyone would be first, he must be last of all and servant of all.'"

Jesus took an authoritative posture of a teacher as he sat down with his twelve disciples surrounding him. He gave them the truth about true greatness; it is not found in being first and served by all, but in being last and a servant to all. An inflated ego (Mark 8:34) finds itself unable and unwilling to pick up a cross. In an endearing object lesson, Jesus took a child, who represented those with no power, no status, and few rights, and hugged him—hugs of attention and acceptance. His listeners and observers were to exhibit these same traits.

Mark 10:35–45:

And James and John, the sons of Zebedee, came up to him and said to him, "Teacher, we want you to do for us whatever we ask of you." And he said to them, "What do you want me to do for you?" And they said to him, "Grant us to sit, one at your right hand and one at your left, in your glory." Jesus said to them, "You do not know what you are asking. Are you able to drink

the cup that I drink, or to be baptized with the baptism with which I am baptized?" And they said to him, "We are able." And Jesus said to them, "The cup that I drink you will drink, and with the baptism with which I am baptized, you will be baptized, but to sit at my right hand or at my left is not mine to grant, but it is for those for whom it has been prepared." And when the ten heard it, they began to be indignant at James and John. And Jesus called them to him and said to them, "You know that those who are considered rulers of the Gentiles lord it over them, and their great ones exercise authority over them. But it shall not be so among you. But whoever would be great among you must be your servant, and whoever would be first among you must be slave of all. For even the Son of Man came not to be served but to serve, and to give his life as a ransom for many."

Mark depicts Jesus as the Servant of Yahweh, a fulfillment of the suffering servant prophesied in Isaiah 52:13–53:12. In a culture that highly regarded honor and sought to avoid shame at all costs, Jesus' teaching and demonstration of the leader as a servant were unwelcome. In contrast to the cultural standards of Roman social life, in God's kingdom the radical nature of sacrificial service was the true sign of greatness. While one of his greatest demonstrations of the leader as a servant was the washing of his disciples' feet, Jesus' ultimate example of servant leadership was his suffering, crucifixion, and death. Jesus' life would become a *ransom* for others, a word that meant the price paid to release a slave or captive from bondage.

Luke 7:41–47:

"A certain moneylender had two debtors. One owed five hundred denarii, and the other fifty. When they could not pay, he cancelled the debt of both. Now which of them will love him more?" Simon answered, "The one, I suppose, for whom he cancelled the larger debt." And he said to him, "You have judged rightly." Then turning toward the woman he said to Simon, "Do you see this woman? I entered your house; you gave me no water for my feet, but she has wet my feet with her tears and wiped them with her hair. You gave me no kiss, but from the time I came in she has not ceased to kiss my feet. You did not anoint my head with oil, but she has anointed my feet with ointment. Therefore I tell you, her sins, which are many, are forgiven—for she loved much. But he who is forgiven little, loves little."

This passage is not often understood as describing service, but it should be. As a result of having received forgiveness for many sins, this woman with a tarnished reputation demonstrated her love for Jesus. She washed Jesus' feet with her tears; whereas, Simon, a Pharisee, failed to offer the customary water for footwashing. She kissed Jesus' feet; whereas, Simon refused to offer a traditional kiss of welcome. She anointed Jesus' feet with a rare, expensive perfume; whereas, Simon omitted the conventional olive oil, plentiful and cheap. Simon's inhospitality sharply contrasted with the woman's love as expressed in serving and honoring Jesus.

Luke 10:25–37:

And behold, a lawyer stood up to put him to the test, saying, "Teacher, what shall I do to inherit eternal life?" He said to him, "What is written in the Law? How do you read it?" And he answered, "You shall love the Lord your God with all your heart and with all your soul and with all your strength and with all your mind, and your neighbor as yourself." And he said to him, "You have answered correctly; do this, and you will live."

But he, desiring to justify himself, said to Jesus, "And who is my neighbor?" Jesus replied, "A man was going down from Jerusalem to Jericho, and he fell among robbers, who stripped him and beat him and departed, leaving him half dead. Now by chance a priest was going down that road, and when he saw him he passed by on the other side. So likewise a Levite, when he came to the place and saw him, passed by on the other side. But a Samaritan, as he journeyed, came to where he was, and when he saw him, he had compassion. He went to him and bound up his wounds, pouring on oil and wine. Then he set him on his own animal and brought him to an inn and took care of him. And the next day he took out two denarii and gave them to the innkeeper, saying, 'Take care of him, and whatever more you spend, I will repay you when I come back.' Which of these three, do you think, proved to be a neighbor to the man who fell among the robbers?" He said, "The one who showed him mercy." And Jesus said to him, "You go, and do likewise."

The practice of loving God and neighbor would have been familiar to the listeners of Jesus' exchange with the lawyer; it was part of the Old Testament law. When this expert confronted Jesus to test his credibility, the tables turned and he became the object of inquiry. The lawyer's response to Jesus' question incorporated part of the Shema (Deuteronomy 6:5), which is a daily call to love God with all our being, and part of Leviticus 19:18, which speaks of loving our neighbor. What started as a theological question turned into practical life issues. The lawyer was not fully satisfied with this answer. He wanted Jesus to distinguish who constitutes a neighbor, hoping, perhaps, to narrow the field of those he would be responsible to love.

The parable presents a man traveling a treacherous seventeen-mile stretch of road lined with caves perfect for housing thieves and robbers. The man is nearly beaten to death. The expected heroes of the story would have been the theologians of the day—the priest and the scribe. But they fail miserably. The hero is a Samaritan, a half-breed who is considered unclean simply because he is not a Jew. The Samaritan extends compassion beyond what is expected. Jesus' answer to "Who is my neighbor?" is "You be the neighbor." The focus is not on who our neighbor is but on how we are to be a neighbor to those in need. Whereas, we would want to filter people out, limiting those we are to serve, Jesus would ask, "Whom have you served today?" Those in need come in unexpected sizes, shapes, and colors. So do neighbors.

John 13:3–5 and 1 John 3:16–18:

Jesus, knowing that the Father had given all things into his hands, and that he had come from God and was going back to God, rose from supper. He laid aside his outer garments, and taking a towel, tied it around his waist. Then he poured water into a basin and began to wash the disciples' feet and to wipe them with the towel that was wrapped around him. (John 13: 3–5)

By this we know love, that he laid down his life for us, and we ought to lay down our lives for the brothers. But if anyone has the world's goods and sees his brother in need, yet closes his heart against him, how does God's love abide in him? Little children, let us not love in word or talk but in deed and in truth. (1 John 3:16–18)

Regarding the phrases "laid aside his outer garments" and "taking a towel," the exact Greek wording is "lay down" and "take up." These are the same works Jesus used when speaking of laying down his life at the cross and taking it up again. In 1 John when we *take up* service, we are essentially dying to self! The truest evidence that God abides in a redeemed soul is the outward expression of loving others.

Romans 12:11: "Do not be slothful in zeal, be fervent in spirit, serve the Lord."

Serving God should be a picture of enthusiasm, earnestness, and diligence. A slothful response is incompatible with the rightful response to the giver of abundant life.

Ephesians 4:11–12: "And he gave the apostles, the prophets, the evangelists, the shepherds and teachers, to equip the saints for the work of ministry, for building up the body of Christ."

These given gifts of ministry describe the role of leaders as that of equipping God's people in building up the body of Christ. The internal strength of the church, the body of Christ, is girded by the service of the saints.

Ephesians 6:6–7: "Not by the way of eye-service, as people-pleasers, but as servants of Christ, doing the will of God from the heart, rendering service with a good will as to the Lord and not to man."

The condition of the heart is more clearly reflected in its motivation for serving than in the action of serving. A heart masquerade may fool people, but not God. The One who knows you to the core is the One who sees your service from the inside out.

Colossians 3:22–24: "Slaves, obey in everything those who are your earthly masters, not by way of eye-service, as people-pleasers, but with sincerity of heart, fearing the Lord. Whatever you do, work heartily, as for the Lord and not for men, knowing that from the Lord you will receive the inheritance as your reward. You are serving the Lord Christ."

"Whatever you do" transcends our employment status and extends to *any* activity we engage in. The all-knowing God is always concerned with how well we do our work. Ultimately, God will reward us for our earthly labors, regardless of how we are recompensed in this life.

James 2:14–17: "What good is it, my brothers, if someone

says he has faith but does not have works? Can that faith save him? If a brother or sister is poorly clothed and lacking in daily food, and one of you says to them, 'Go in peace, be warmed and filled,' without giving them the things needed for the body, what good is that? So also faith by itself, if it does not have works, is dead."

This is the first of four vignettes James used to show that faith without works is counterfeit faith—a false faith that will not save a person. Notice how the word *good* bookends this passage. What "good" is there in praying for the welfare of the poor and yet doing nothing about it? This excuse simply conceals the underlying prideful refusal to place self aside for the benefit of another.

1 Peter 2:16–17: "Live as people who are free, not using your freedom as a cover-up for evil, but living as servants of God. Honor everyone. Love the brotherhood. Fear God. Honor the emperor."

This passage contains a seeming oxymoron: living free as a servant. True freedom doesn't conceal; it reveals. The freedom to serve God shows up in honoring all people and loving one another. This was a tall order in light of the horrific persecution Peter and his readers endured under the emperor.

1 Peter 4:10: "As each has received a gift, use it to serve one another, as good stewards of God's varied grace."

Every Spirit-given gift is to be used in community, exemplifying a broad spectrum of God's grace.

Food for Thought

There are service stations, service industries, service centers, and service contracts. There is self-service, customer service, and full service. What is consistent with these is that, as consumers, we are the recipients of such services. To be on the receiving end of service is the preferred, privileged side. Time and effort are

liberally spent on establishing and securing our position on this side of receiving. Advertisers know this is so. Read a few ads and see for yourself:

- "Talk at will. Text at will. Connect at will." (Verizon)
- "Makin' it easy, easy on you." (Toyota)
- "I'm lovin' it." (McDonald's)
- "Have it your way." (Burger King)

When presented with an opportunity to serve, often we are glad if it is a one-shot, short-term deal that promises not to rob us of much time, attention, or energy. It may be just enough of an effortless self-promotion point to impress someone or to build a resumé.

Those who perform menial tasks are often regarded as personal staff, readily available at another's beck and call. These people are typically marginalized, ignored, or abused. Being a servant or slave was the lowest rung on the first-century Greco-Roman social ladder. The economic stability of the ancient world was driven by slavery. Either because they were prisoners of war or because they were in economic debt, men and women became slaves. It was characterized by obedience and selfless devotion committed to seeking the benefit of another. No one freely chose to be a servant or slave.

Yet, this is exactly what Jesus did. He took on the very nature of a servant (Philippians 2:7). In a power-conscious world, he donned the towel of the gospel. The servant Messiah washed the feet of his disciples on the night before his crucifixion (John 13). The picture is powerful, the act perplexing, the moment recorded.

I've participated in a number of footwashing ceremonies as a server and as a recipient, each one a moving experience. But none compared to the one I had the opportunity to observe as my colleague set up bowls of water with sets of towels to wash the feet of willing students. Jim was my boss, the chair of the Biblical and Theological Studies Department, and his diagnosis of malignant brain cancer was only one month old. He entered the classroom

early that March morning. His symptoms were overt. He tired easily and was navigated around to this class session in a wheelchair. His speech was slow, but his intent strong. His students read passages from John 13 as PowerPoint slides rotated across the screen. Images of Ford Madox Brown's *Jesus Washing Peter's Feet* visually drew the students into the act taking place before them.

I took note of Jim's brief conversation with each student and wondered what Jesus might have said to his disciples as he held each foot close, rubbed the dirt and grime from its calloused crevices, and soothed each with a gentle embrace. He knew what each would face in the critical days and nights ahead. Did he look into each of his disciples' eyes? Did he assure each disciple of his unique gift? Did he encourage them to stay the course? Did he challenge them to trust him, knowing the unfolding challenges of the next seventy-two hours? Scripture is silent on this.

If there was a way for my students to sense this aspect of Jesus, I wanted that for them. Every semester since that spring day I have donned the towel of the gospel and knelt before an empty chair. Each of my synchronized PowerPoint slides takes its turn on the screen even as the visual silence is broken by the first students who are either courageous or curious enough to find themselves in the seat before me. I hold their feet, rub the dirt and grime from each, and soothe each with a gentle embrace. As I do so, I call their names, look into their eyes, and wait to convey a word or message that God may have laid on my heart for them. The experience is powerful.

How To

One of the best ways to develop a lifestyle of servanthood is to be mindful of what Christ has already done in his greatest act of sacrificial service in the giving of his life for ours. Then in response, start each day with a prayer: Help me to be sensitive to the ways you are growing a serving heart in me.

Cultivating the heart of a Spirit-filled servant is more pleasing to God than a life of service activities.

Pitfalls

Earning

It is an easy and subtle temptation to perceive our serving God as a viable way to earn his favor. The false belief that what we do for God influences his love or attention toward us is built on our human predisposition for formulaic cause and effect: if I do this, then God will certainly do that. It is our attempt to manipulate God. We cannot secure a divine insurance policy leveraging our service against the possibility of tragedy or disaster. Evidence of this mindset is revealed when misfortune occurs and we cry out, "Why, God? I have done so much for you." Our "doing" does not impact his love and concern for us; his love for his own is beyond measure and unchanging. We are defined by who we are in Christ, recognized by what we do.

Substitute

It is scriptural that our faith is evidenced in works. Service can be a clear way for server and recipient to see God's Spirit at work. But without a strong working knowledge of God's Word, we can lose the reason, focus, and purpose for serving; our faith become works based and not grace based. This kind of service is a weak substitute for a growing faith.

Slothfulness

Even when we know God's prompting to serve, we still find it far easier to donate money than to get our hands dirty. Which requires more faith? Which will grow our faith? Which would Jesus choose to do? Laziness reveals our pride of entitlement.

Perspective

Some of the greatest acts of service will never get media coverage or earthly recognition. We err in waiting for God to use us in big

ways because it blinds us to seeing the countless people he places right in front of us whom he is calling us to serve. Perhaps one day in heaven we will hear his commendation for a simple act of sharing a meal or patiently listening or giving a timely hug. Our sad reply might be, "Oh, Lord, I could have done more of that." The heart of service is relational.

God's Stirring

What becomes more and more apparent is our shrinking need for recognition. We begin to see what is important in God's kingdom; it will always be about people. Service isn't measured by the "bigness" or smallness; it is measured by the lifestyle humility that is grown through serving others and allowing others to serve us. Service is the avenue for pleasing God. A lifestyle of service is taking root when it is enough to know that God sees and is pleased with the responsive heart that fuels the hands that serve. These are precursors to hearing that ultimate praise: "Well done, good and faithful servant."

Reflections from the Heart

• When our professor washed the feet of some of the students in our class, I decided to wash the feet of someone who would probably not want me to and who I would feel it hard to do for. This person was my father. My father and I have a history of not agreeing on much and constantly arguing and not really getting along. We never really became that close, but now we have been bridging the gap between us, so I thought that this would be a great humbling experience for me, and also something that might give him and me something to bond with and hopefully show a side of my Christian walk.

I told him that I needed him to complete a homework assignment, but did not tell him at first what it was. He agreed to help me complete it, and later in the day, I told him that

what I needed to do was wash his feet in the presence of my younger brother and sister and mother. He agreed, though I could tell that he felt a bit weird about it. I remembered what Foster said about self-righteous service and how this type of service expected a reward for performing the service. This is why I chose to wash his feet and tell him about Jesus doing it and reading from the Bible so to give him this and not expect anything in return. I knelt down and told my family why Jesus did it and read from the Bible what he said. They listened, and I told them that in those days slaves washed the feet of people, so for Jesus to humble himself and serve others in this way is a great indicator as to how much Jesus values service. This is why if we believe in God, I told them, we should follow his example and not worry about how things might seem to other people, but only concern ourselves with what our Lord desires from us. Sometimes our pride or concern for how we will appear to others may keep us from serving, but if Jesus did it and said he expects us to do it, why should we feel that we cannot give this small gesture of humility toward others? *David L.*

- I feel I also need to admit my reluctance to be served. I often prefer giving than receiving. This is not to say there is never a thought about receiving something in return for what I do, whether it be blessing from God or reciprocation or at least appreciation from people, but I try not to entertain those thoughts for long. I believe this is right, for my motivation should never be for what I can get. But I have also become unable and almost antagonistic toward receiving gifts or service from other people, such as someone paying for my meal, for instance. I am not completely sure what the reason is. I feel some of it may be because I do not like attention, which is true, but I know a lot of it is also pride, which I am sad to admit. I feel like I can take care of myself, and I do not like

the feeling of needing to owe someone. But now I know I have refused service at the cost of rejecting a person's love. I am suddenly hit with the realization that refusing this love through service is not seeking selflessness but actually practicing selfishness, when I try to love but refuse to receive it. How can I do this and expect to foster relationship? And how is this living in the light of God's love, which, eternally bountiful, has been bestowed upon me? I do not deserve that, yet I have received it. Unless I am wrong, clearly my idea of love has been shortsighted. *Jeff S.*

- I prayed about service and how God could show me how to serve better, and he brought me great circumstances in a few days. My close and dear friend was experiencing a trial that was not easy for her to go through, and I prayed about how I could serve her in her time of need. God answered me with the silence. He told me to listen to her and allow her to pour her heart out to me. As I humbled my heart and listened to her instead of my putting in my boastful advice, I was able to really feel the heart of my dear friend. *Brooklin B.*

- As I was walking to the bus stop, I saw these two middle-aged women trying to push a dead car into a parking space. They were somewhat in the way of traffic, and they couldn't get the car to budge. I was pretty far from the scene, and as I watched, heading in their direction, I waited to see if anyone was going to help. This was around a high school, and there were several students exiting school, scattered around the street. I decided that if no one helped them by the time I got there, then I would help them myself. Well, it turns out that no one did help them, and I asked the two ladies if I could help. They said yes, and I began to push the car out to the curb. I'm not going to lie; I was a little embarrassed because people were watching us push the car, and it was a little weird being surrounded by a bunch of high school students. I actually

felt a little uncool, which I am rather ashamed to say. But that's the thing. I actually didn't mind being in that position. After I helped the ladies, I said, "Dios te bendiga," which means "God bless you" in Spanish (they were Hispanic). And I was rather surprised when they returned the same as well and said thank you. That situation put a smile to my face, and as I walked on, I could not help but feel really happy. That's why I didn't mind feeling a little uncool. This service really did help me grow in humility. I was able to set aside my "mask" of pride and simply help the two ladies in need. It's actually hard for me to do that sometimes. In theory, helping two ladies push a car doesn't sound bad at all. But when there are people watching, your pride actually clouds your judgment and tells you not to help others because it puts you in a position of inferiority and people are watching you make a fool of yourself, or so that's how it goes. I was kind of close to not helping them, because there were so many people, but I decided to do it because I wanted to help them, regardless if people were watching. *Jesus R.*

• Once I became a Christian, I knew that I was supposed to be a servant. However, I usually don't act like a servant. If there is an opportunity to serve others, I usually avoid eye contact or find an excuse to get out of the extra work. But we are supposed to be part of the ministry of being interrupted. Instead of coming up with excuses of why I can't help, I am now going to sacrifice my pride and time and try to serve others. This weekend I went home and spent some time with my family. Saturday night I was doing my homework when I saw that my mom had started the dishes. However, she had left the kitchen to help my sister in her bedroom. I was reading my homework for this class and was reminded that this week that we were studying service. My first thought was, "Oh no, I don't have time; I have to get this homework

done." But then I remembered that serving is the ministry of being interrupted. I still didn't get up right away, because I had finally settled down and was getting into my work and wanted to get it done. But I couldn't get service off my mind. After a couple of more seconds, I swallowed my pride, walked into the kitchen, and started doing the dishes. When my mom came back out, she thanked me, and I could see how happy she was. Just a simple act of doing the dishes brought a huge smile to my mom's face, and that made the small sacrifice of my time completely worth it. Just this small act of service was tough for me, but it is a start. If I want to show Christ's love to the world, then I need to start living a lifestyle of serving others. *Benji S.*

- When I found out you would be washing our feet, I was taken aback at first. I mean why would you want to wash the feet of your students? I was almost set on not going up because I felt bad that you would have to touch our gross feet. We all know that is how Jesus served his disciples, and most of us keep it a story and don't literally live it out. Washing feet, as we all have heard, is truly one of the most humble tasks one can perform. I found myself almost feeling bad for you that you would have to do this dirty job. But as I was sitting there, thinking this whole thing through, God started speaking to me, I think. It all of sudden hit me that you wanted to do this; you wanted to wash our feet as an act of love to your students. You wanted to show us the same love Christ has clearly poured out onto you. So then I made up my mind—if you wanted to serve me, I wanted to let you serve me; I would go up. I seriously was so nervous. I felt a little embarrassed that you would have to touch my feet, and I had no idea what you meant when you said you would be talking to us. I sat and observed what this all looked like for about half the time and still just felt so uneasy, but at the same time felt so called to go up to you.

I had no idea why this was all such a huge deal to me. I don't understand why I couldn't simply just let you serve me without me feeling so weird about it. It didn't hit me until afterward. As you probably remember, I started crying when you started speaking to me. It didn't take long for the whole waterworks to start. The words you spoke to me honestly hit me in a place so deep I couldn't hold back tears. I definitely did not expect to hear those words. I thought maybe something a little more generic. . . . I had no idea what to expect. I needed to hear those words. I needed to be served in that way. For whatever reason, God knew that this was something that was going to affirm me in a way I would not understand until after it was finished. . . . This was one of those times where he took a situation that was meant to be so simple and so humble, and he used it to transform my heart a little bit more. I have no clue what is in store for me, but I do know that God redefined service for me last week, and I think service will play a huge role in whatever God has planned for my future. *Lindsay S.*

• Honestly, I had absolutely no idea what to expect when I got out of my chair and started walking to the front of the room with the intention of getting my feet washed. But when I sat down, I was met with a very loving smile and words of blessing. The words that were spoken were obviously not a planned speech or simply a "feel-good" message. They were specific and true. They penetrated my exterior and dove right inside of me. The words that were spoken were a tremendous blessing as well. When I went back to my seat after the blessing and the foot washing took place, I could only sit in silence. I needed time to let the words and actions done percolate through my mind. So I sat in quiet meditation for some time. I thought about what a magnificent blessing I had just been given. I thought about how the actions and words I do

and speak affect others. I thought about how I need to continuously remind myself to be a light to this world no matter where I am or what I am doing. *David M.*

Fill in the Blank

Service breaks the seduction of _____ and allows me to hear God's invitation to/for _____.

Closing Thought

We serve because he first served us. The more Jesus' humility finds its home in a servant's heart, the more pride becomes a guest that has overstayed its welcome.

Helpful Reads

Richard Foster, *Celebration of Discipline: The Path to Spiritual Growth* (San Francisco: HarperSanFrancisco, 1998), chapter 9.

Klaus Issler, *Wasting Time with God: A Christian Spirituality of Friendship with God* (Downers Grove: InterVarsity Press, 2001), chapter 3.

John Ortberg, *The Life You've Always Wanted: Spiritual Disciplines for Ordinary People* (Grand Rapids: Zondervan, 2004), chapter 7.

Donald Whitney, *Spiritual Disciplines for the Christian Life* (Colorado Springs: NavPress, 1991), chapter 7.

Dallas Willard, *The Spirit of the Disciplines: Understanding How God Changes Lives* (San Francisco: HarperSanFrancisco, 1991), 182–184.

12
CELEBRATION:
GETTING READY FOR
THE GREATEST PARTY

Definition: The delight-filled response toward God and the world around us prompted by who he is, what he has done, and what he will do.

Letting the Word Speak

Old Testament

Zephaniah 3:17: "The LORD your God is in your midst, a mighty one who will save; he will rejoice over you with gladness; he will quiet you by his love; he will exult over you with loud singing."

The seventeenth verse in this graphic, fifty-three-verse book gives the cause for celebration: "God is in your midst." His love, mentioned only here in the whole of Zephaniah, brings renewal and victory. The people respond in trust and join in song. And God himself joins in, singing loudly in his triumph.

Psalm 16:11: "You make known to me the path of life; in your presence there is fullness of joy; at your right hand are pleasures forevermore."

Simple words for the path of life describe its leading into

eternity and the continued presence of God. The "joys" (literally) and pleasures are found in who God is and what he gives. The refugee in crisis described in verse 1 found himself an heir with an inheritance beyond all imagination. These joys are found in the journey with the Lord and to the Lord.

Psalm 47:1: "Clap your hands, all peoples! Shout to God with loud songs of joy!"

The superscription notes this is a psalm "of the sons of Korah." Korah was an ancestor of a group of musicians placed in charge of temple worship by King David and King Solomon. "Clap your hands" is a clasping of others' hands in an act of unity and in joyous response to God. The psalmist called all nations to come into agreement regarding their relationship to Yahweh. There will be a party of global proportions.

Psalm 150:
> Praise the LORD!
> Praise God in his sanctuary;
>> praise him in his mighty heavens!
> Praise him for his mighty deeds;
>> praise him according to his excellent greatness!
> Praise him with trumpet sound;
>> praise him with lute and harp!
> Praise him with tambourine and dance;
>> praise him with strings and pipe!
> Praise him with sounding cymbals;
>> praise him with loud clashing cymbals!
> Let everything that has breath praise the LORD!
> Praise the LORD!

The book of Psalms is divided into five collections (1–41; 42–72; 73–89; 90–106; and 107–150), and each one closes with a doxology. The last five psalms (Psalms 146–150) are "Hallelujah" psalms that serve to remind God's people of his ultimate

sovereignty. The very last psalm, quoted above, brings the entire Psalter to an end with calls to praise with song and dance. All theology leads to doxology.

Isaiah 55:12: "For you shall go out in joy and be led forth in peace; the mountains and the hills before you shall break forth into singing, and all the trees of the field shall clap their hands."

Isaiah wrote of God's sovereign majesty and redemptive love as revealed in his interactions with the Israelites. Their return to the Lord (and from exile) led to the return to their land. Those who were once so far from God were restored to his peace and fellowship. Imagine mountains breaking forth in singing and trees clapping their hands as signs of great joy at sinners being made holy through the Word of God. Now that's exuberant joy.

New Testament

Luke 15:7, 10: "Just so, I tell you, there will be more joy in heaven over one sinner who repents than over ninety-nine righteous persons who need no repentance. . . . Just so, I tell you, there is joy before the angels of God over one sinner who repents."

Jesus spent time sharing the gospel with tax collectors and sinners, but the religious leaders of the day would not associate with those who did not keep the law. Jesus was more concerned with befriending the lost than offending the pious. Luke records Jesus' teaching of three lost possessions: a sheep, a coin, and a son. The Messiah began with, "Suppose one of you" (NIV) or "What man of you," asking each to engage in the story as a virtual participant. As the listeners resonated with the shepherd in the first parable, who celebrated with friends and neighbors over finding the one lost sheep, so they understood the cause for joy over finding the lost coin. However the Pharisees had grumbled about Jesus finding lost people, because they did not consider these reprobates valuable. There was a Jewish saying that spoke of their mindset: "There is joy before God when those who provoke him perish

from the world." Jesus corrected this view of God in describing God's great delight when a repenting sinner is found. The resulting joy of heaven is compared to a great party. Oh, how heaven parties!

1 Corinthians 11:26: "For as often as you eat this bread and drink the cup, you proclaim the Lord's death until he comes."

Jesus made the simple elements of a meal to mean something divine. Christians celebrate Jesus' death and his return in the Lord's Supper or Communion. His shed blood is evidence that he accepted the wrath of God you and I deserved. Jesus made it possible to know and have peace with God. We who have moved from death to life celebrate regularly and with soul-deep conviction, remembering he died, he is risen, and he is coming again.

Revelation: 5:9–10:

And they sang a new song, saying,

"Worthy are you to take the scroll
    and to open its seals,
for you were slain, and by your blood you ransomed
people for God
    from every tribe and language and people and
nation,
and you have made them a kingdom and priests to
our God,
    and they shall reign on the earth."

The "new song"—a theme that continues from the Old Testament (Psalm 98:1; Isaiah 42:10)—celebrates the divine deliverance and defeat of evil and sin through Jesus Christ. By virtue of his death and resurrection, the Lamb is worthy to take the scroll and open its seals. The effective salvific work of the Lamb reaches every corner of the earth. Followers of the Lamb corporately become a kingdom and individually become priests, worshiping him in the new kingdom of God.

Revelation 19:1–7:

After this I heard what seemed to be the loud voice of a great multitude in heaven, crying out,

"Hallelujah!
Salvation and glory and power belong to our God,
    for his judgments are true and just;
for he has judged the great prostitute
    who corrupted the earth with her immorality,
and has avenged on her the blood of his servants."

Once more they cried out,

"Hallelujah!
The smoke from her goes up forever and ever."

And the twenty-four elders and the four living creatures fell down and worshiped God who was seated on the throne, saying, "Amen. Hallelujah!" And from the throne came a voice saying,

"Praise our God,
    all you his servants,
you who fear him,
    small and great."

Then I heard what seemed to be the voice of a great multitude, like the roar of many waters and like the sound of mighty peals of thunder, crying out,

"Hallelujah!
For the Lord our God
    the Almighty reigns.
Let us rejoice and exult
    and give him the glory,
for the marriage of the Lamb has come,
    and his Bride has made herself ready."

Hallelujah is a common word in religious vocabulary and means "praise God," and Revelation is the only place in the New Testament where this word is found. The heavenly angels praise God because salvation, glory, and power belong to him. He has exercised his just and true judgment on the great harlot who corrupted the world. God has brought the downfall of evil.

The second "Hallelujah" response comes from the elders and living creatures and is repeated again as the saints on earth join in praising God. In the fourth and final "Hallelujah," the multitude calls all God's people, heavenly and earthly, to "rejoice and exult."

Matthew 5:12 tells the persecuted saints to "rejoice and be glad, for your reward is great in heaven." The psalmists told the people to rejoice and be glad (Psalms 31:7; 32:11; 70:4; 118:24), and the Chronicler in 1 Chronicles 16:31 added, "The LORD reigns!" The reason for the joy lies in God's eternal reign that is beginning to come in its fullness and in the wedding of the Lamb. Believers are the bride of Christ, and the wedding day has come.

Revelation 19:9: "And the angel said to me, 'Write this: Blessed are those who are invited to the marriage supper of the Lamb.' And he said to me, 'These are the true words of God.'"

The theme of marriage between God and his people is found woven through the Old Testament in the writing prophets Hosea, Isaiah, and Jeremiah. It continues in the Gospels (Matthew, Mark, and John) and the Epistles (Ephesians and 2 Corinthians). Finally, in Revelation the wedding feast reveals the final triumph of Jesus Christ and pictures the character of our relationship with him: committed love, intimate communion, exuberant joy, and unwavering fidelity.

Revelation 21:3–4: "And I heard a loud voice from the throne saying, 'Behold, the dwelling place of God is with man. He will dwell with them, and they will be his people, and God himself will be with them as their God. He will wipe away every

tear from their eyes, and death shall be no more, neither shall there be mourning, nor crying, nor pain anymore, for the former things have passed away.'"

God has been looking forward to this for a long time. He will finally and eternally have his place among his people. His "dwelling" or "tabernacle" comes associated with John 1:14 where "the Word became flesh and dwelt [tabernacled] among us." As the saints who inhabit the new heaven and new earth enjoy the peace and joy God gives his people, the tears shed from suffering and sacrifice are wiped away by God himself. He will remove every source of sorrow, and in its place will be total bliss and profound delight. Death, the final enemy, with all its associates, is destroyed. The real party continues in full force.

Food for Thought

Happiness was considered a virtue in ancient times. Nowadays it has become a goal. We tend to look for external factors to make us happy: a job, a new car, a different house, dark chocolate, a pay raise, a puppy, a vacation, or things going our way. Seeking happiness in things reveals its fickleness. There is often a diminishing return—things that once brought us happiness do not continue to do so. This can create a constant search for new sources of happiness, while we grow inattentive to the things that bring deep joy. Happiness is often mistaken for joy. Happiness skips along the surface of the heart; whereas, joy resides deep within.

Because God invented joy, it is found woven throughout his Word. In the Old Testament joy is most often associated with celebrating the gracious acts of God toward Israel. The most logical responses to God's intervening on behalf of his people were celebrations of remembrance. Abounding joy continues through the Gospel accounts of Jesus' birth, triumphal entry, and resurrection. The authors of the Acts and a number of the Epistles wrote of joy to the churches scattered throughout the first-century world.

In Revelation we find the ultimate joy and celebration in

heaven described. Weddings were, and still are, public and festive occasions. Believers, as the glorious bride of Christ, join the Lamb at the wedding feast (Revelation 19:9; Isaiah 25:6). This is *the* destination wedding of all time and eternity. John's readers would have received much-needed comfort from his entire letter. Their joy was to be grounded in knowing that God is sovereign, Jesus is victorious, and his salvation for them was certain. These joyful truths were to impact how they reacted to their present circumstances.

Reflecting on the joy in our lives requires time and thought, commodities we extend more freely to short-term, self-fulfilling activities. Joy is a quality, a gift, grounded in and derived from God himself. The thrilling truth of being known by God is to reside so deep in our hearts that even when circumstances change, our joy doesn't. His joy is found in us knowing him in the deepest parts of our souls and our living the gift of his salvation. It may take a bit of recalibrating when matters of the soul are disrupted, but joy remains at the core of our inmost being and insists on bubbling to the top. The option of joyless, shriveled souls does not exist because the reason for divine joy is ever present and unchanging. It is simple and deep and is intricately connected with our relationship with God and others.

Through a variety of means, God gives us grace to grow and opportunities to celebrate. We become participants in the joy-yielding process of spiritual transformation.

- Through *getting into his Word* I celebrate the grace of God's redemptive plan.
- Through *meditating on his Word* I celebrate the grace that I am part of his redemptive plan.
- Through *silence and solitude* I celebrate the grace of his nearness.
- Through *fasting* I celebrate that the grace of his sufficiency.
- Through *prayer* I celebrate the grace of his voice.

- Through *confession* I celebrate the grace of his all-encompassing forgiveness.
- Through *conference* I celebrate the grace of his community.
- Through the *sacred night of the soul* I celebrate the grace of his presence.
- Through *biblical hospitality* I celebrate the grace of his friendship.
- Through *thanksgiving* I celebrate the grace of his *hesed*.
- Through *service* I celebrate the grace of his humility.
- Through *celebration* I celebrate the grace of his complete joy.

A joy-filled life is one that is changed. If you want to know what it looks like, you may be asking the wrong question. The appearance of happiness can be quite deceitful. Many who appear happy can actually be joy deficient. Joy may show up in exuberant celebration, but not necessarily. External perceptions can be inferior indications of a person's joy quotient. Certainly, joy can be expressed in outward acts of delight and pleasure or with an overt bubbly zest for life, but it is best recognized in conversations between those who care to know us. The most serious of people can be the most joyful, but we may never know that without hearing their stories.

Celebration, then, is the life attitude of the inward joy that accompanies us on our walk with God and others. Celebration is evidence that the Holy Spirit is at work in a person's heart. Whereas happiness strives to avoid situations of sadness, joy is a comforting and comfortable presence even when trials come. Joy can make its most profound presence in the face of sorrow.

And if you need a reminder of joy-causing celebration, consider the regular reminders God has ordained for us in sharing Communion or the Lord's Supper, as Paul described it in 1 Corinthians 11:20. *Eucharistia* is the Greek word from which we get *Eucharist*, otherwise known as Communion. It means

"grateful" or "thankful." The first Communion was celebrated at the Last Supper, where the bread and wine, picturing Jesus' body and blood, were given and consumed in remembrance of Jesus' death. Paul said to keep doing this, keep remembering Jesus' sacrifice, until he returns, because he is going to return.

Jesus' death by crucifixion was gruesome. As horrific as this was, it gave only a glimpse of the spiritual suffering endured by Christ. Yet for the joy set before him, he endured it (Hebrews 12:2). For the joy and pleasure of the Father's exalting and enthroning him, for the completed joy of victory over death for those he loved and had to leave behind, for the joy of being with the Father as they had been throughout eternity past, Jesus endured the cross. His joy is ours to "enjoy" in anticipation of the consummation of God's kingdom.

When joy resides in the heart, there is a freedom that allows us to enjoy all those things that make us happy and to heartily celebrate those things with others as well. But when we seek personal fulfillment and happiness as a goal, joy will be elusive. When we seek joy, happiness comes along for the ride. Joy radiates and fuels celebration of the grandest kind, and celebration then becomes our new normal.

How To

Create a column of things that make you happy. These usually come to mind quickly and without much effort. Next, create a column of things that bring you deep joy. This list will require more time and thought than the first. After completing both, meet together with a good friend and review your entries. Be prepared to add to your lists. Reflect together with some honest questions:

- Does my life reflect one of celebration?
- If so, what conversations reflect that truth?
- If not, why not?
- How do I react to other people's happiness or joy?
- How does the truth of knowing who God is and what

he has done compete with thoughts of pursuing my own personal happiness?

- Do my checkbook and daily schedules reflect more the busyness, productivity, and accumulation of things or the importance of relationships?
- How have I let someone or something rob me of the joy God has given?
- What does it look like when I forget the joy God has placed deep within the wells of my soul?
- When was the last time I thought about Jesus' coming again, his victory over death and sin, and how he has invited me to his wedding feast?
- How might these truths impact how I live today?

Pitfalls

Entanglement

The world inundates us with messages that purposefully promote selfishness and greed. The fallen world system wants nothing more than for human beings to be convinced that engaging in the game of comparison, which propels the drive to acquire more at any cost, can bring happiness. True joy transforms the propensity toward self-fulfillment and constant comparing into an ability to enjoy God's blessings with a pure heart.

Battle

Joy must be guarded. Those who would desire to sabotage this confidence seem intent on belittling our joy for the purpose of exalting their own achievements. It is in times like these that we must hear God say, "Don't let anyone or anything rob you of the joy I've given you." This joy is grounded in the truth and certainty of the present and future hope in Christ. A God-honoring response will be the most effective device that, while guarding your heart, gives evidence of the strength of your faith.

Self-Condemnation

Some people think they don't deserve to celebrate, to be joyful or even happy. They falsely believe this is reserved for those who live the perfect life. Unconfessed sin, harbored unforgiveness, and self-imposed condemnation hide the truth that God esteemed us before we were born and created within us the need to worship and celebrate. And it is just like God to provide a way for us to be freed from the grasp of sin, unforgiveness, and blame. Look to the cross.

God's Stirring

Because there is freedom in knowing and experiencing God's joy, smiles appear more readily. They are generated by God stirring his joy within our souls. The push of competition and comparison is purged; we can sincerely celebrate when others express joy and happiness.

Our conversations with others reflect this. We speak more often of what God is doing in our lives. Words flow more freely as we inquire of others and we respond to God's goodness. Whether in speech, action, or attitude, a Spirit-prompted outlook on life brings about celebration.

Reflections from the Heart

- Was I a joyful person? I knew that God had designed me to be, and I learned that he *wants* me to be, so if I'm not, I'm not really progressing as well as I could. . . . Celebration is a *spiritual discipline*! That just blew my mind. So I began to let God work in me as I asked myself, "Am I a joyful person?" My heart ached as the Holy Spirit allowed me to be honest with myself: no, I'm really not a joyful person at all. In fact, I'm quite the opposite; I'm really quite a negative and pessimistic person. My heart ached because I realized that my indulging in these feelings was wrong and against what God wanted. I sat there in my room and realized how much I gripped onto my sorrow and negativity even after acknowledging that I *needed* to be joyful, I needed to celebrate. I am so thankful that the Holy Spirit allowed me to have a mirror up to my heart this whole time so that I was not deceived, but it was painful to see the truth. I looked into the mirror in horror as I saw my heart saying, "No, God! I will not enjoy the world around me that you created and you yourself get joy out of! No! I am not going to be happy! I am going to cling to my sadness and never appreciate what you made; it's not worth it! I don't care if I'm suppose to 'celebrate'; I won't!" Oh, the pain in my soul when I saw the wicked rebellion and horrible affinity I had grown for the sin of lack of celebration. However, the battle between my wicked heart and newly created heart by God was a good thing, especially now that I was not being deceived in this area any longer by myself. I then prayed that God would help me with his Holy Spirit and power to overcome this obstacle and to continue overcoming it. I *choose* to celebrate; my wicked heart will not deceive me in shadows anymore—I *choose* to be joyful! God, help me; I don't want to be that way anymore; I want to be like you—joyful. Then, as I allowed God to help me and I made the choice to struggle against my sadness, I noticed just how many things I had to be joyful about. *Megan C.*

- *Celebrating* is a word that is distorted in our culture, but one that its true meaning is necessary. We think of celebrating as partying and not thinking. But really, it's considering God and letting the reality of that birth joy. *Jordan N.*

- It is so strengthening and encouraging to recognize how much God has blessed me—there is so much to celebrate. Yet, I struggle because I feel as though I do not deserve to celebrate because I have not been obedient enough to him. Do I, can I, celebrate despite what I have done or failed to do? God is truly a good God—that is reason to celebrate! *Jamie K.*

Things that make me happy:
- ☐ Friends
- ☐ Hanging out
- ☐ Living in a nice house
- ☐ Reading a good book
- ☐ Spending quality time with someone
- ☐ Wearing something that I like
- ☐ Eating at a restaurant that serves delicious food
- ☐ My dog
- ☐ Watching a fun/good movie
- ☐ Learning body worship
- ☐ Resting at home with my family
- ☐ Looking forward to having a car soon
- ☐ When my room is clean

Things that bring me joy:
- ☐ Knowing that I belong to God
- ☐ Knowing that God loves me no matter what I do or what I am like
- ☐ Knowing that I was made by God, and he made me just the way he wants me to be
- ☐ Praising
- ☐ Knowing that God used me to reach out to someone/ serve others
- ☐ Unconditional love
- ☐ Looking forward to my eternal home
- ☐ Looking forward to how God will use me for the rest of my life/my future
- ☐ Learning to submit to God's will
- ☐ Learning to live through God's testing of my faith

Rachel K.

Fill in the Blank

Celebration breaks the seduction of _____ and allows me to hear God's invitation to/for _____.

Closing Thought

Celebration is becoming of Christians because they, of all the people on earth, know the joy of being known by the Creator of the universe, the Father who delights in giving good gifts to his children.

Helpful Reads

Richard Foster, *Celebration of Discipline: The Path to Spiritual Growth* (San Francisco: HarperSanFrancisco, 1998), chapter 13.

John Ortberg, *The Life You've Always Wanted: Spiritual Disciplines for Ordinary People* (Grand Rapids: Zondervan, 2004), chapter 4.

Dallas Willard, *The Spirit of the Disciplines: Understanding How God Changes Lives* (San Francisco: HarperSanFrancisco, 1991), 179–181.

CONCLUSION

To pen concluding remarks seems almost incongruous, as if, now that we've reached the end of this book, we've arrived at the finish line, or as if the work of spiritual transformation has been done and we can move on to other things in life. If so, then the intent of this book has been missed. Perhaps this section would be more appropriately titled "The Journey Continues." The subtitle of this book is *Cultivating a Lifestyle of Godliness*. The word *cultivating* means improving something by labor and care in order to foster growth. To cultivate a lifestyle of godliness requires a sustained development, a lifelong engagement of learning about and leaning on God. It requires responding to his invitations, hearing his voice, understanding his ways, and capturing the pleasures of being with God in the day-by-day moments of our lives. Those times often catch us midstep as we move along in our day, and in response we briefly pause to absorb the nearness and pleasure of our Creator and Father.

The means of grace are invitations extended by a loving God who desires that his people know more of his presence, more of his grace. To respond to and then know more of his divine grace in our lives changes us—less tin, more tinder. The hardened heart is softened; the distracted soul is nourished; and we, as gracious recipients of an outstanding love, become more like the One who once walked this earth to reveal a Father whose love, commitment,

and power are real. As readied recipients of divine grace, we can become more like Christ.

The journey indeed continues. Look around—there are those who have been placed on the journey with you. They are companions. Look up, to your side, and within. The One who is so lovingly devoted to your growth in godliness is right there with you. And he always will be.

ENDNOTES

Introduction: Stirred Chocolate Milk

1. Jeffrey P. Greenman, "Spiritual Formation in Theological Perspective" in *Life in the Spirit: Spiritual Formation in Theological Perspective*, eds. Jeffrey P. Greenman and George Kalantzis (Downers Grove: InterVarsity Press, 2009), 24.

2. J. I. Packer, *Keep in Step with the Spirit* (Old Tappan, NJ: Fleming H. Revell Company, 1984), 31.

3. C. S. Lewis, *Mere Christianity* (New York: Simon & Schuster Inc., 1943; reprint, New York: Scribner, 1997), 148.

4. John Preston, *Saints' Spirituall Strength* (London: 1637), 113–14.

Chapter 1: Getting into the Word

1. C. S. Lewis, *Reflections on the Psalms* (New York: Harcourt, Brace, 1958), 63.

Chapter 2: The Word Getting into Us

1. Eugene Peterson, *The Message Remix* (Colorado Springs: NavPress, 2003), 16–23.

Chapter 5: Prayer

1. C. S. Lewis, *Letters to Malcolm: Chiefly on Prayer* (New York: Harcourt, Brace & World, 1964), 90.

Chapter 7: Conference

1. Thomas Watson, *Heaven Taken by Storm* (London: Printed by R.W., 1670), 71. Watson was a Puritan clergyman (d. 1686).

2. Thomas Watson, *Religion Our True Interest* (London: Printed by J. Astwood, 1682), 91.

3. Nicholas Bownd, *Sabbathum Veteris et Noui Testament* (London: By Felix Kyngston, 1606), 394. Bownd was a Church of England clergyman (d. 1613).

4. Richard Greenham, *Workes* (London: Imprinted by Felix Kingston, 1605), 227. Greenham was a Church of England clergyman (early 1540s–1594).

5. Matthew Henry, *Matthew Henry's Commentary on the Whole Bible*, vol. 4. (Peabody, MA: Hendrickson Publishers, 1991), 1181–82.

6. Richard Baxter, *The Reformed Pastor*, ed. William Brown (Carlisle, PA: Banner of Truth Trust, 2001), 228. Baxter (1615–1691) was an ejected minister and religious writer.

7. Thomas Watson, *Heaven Taken by Storm* (London: Printed by R.W., 1670), 74.

8. Richard Sibbes, *Bowels Opened* (London: Printed by R. Cotes, 1648), 297. Sibbes (1577–1635) was a Church of England clergyman.

9. John Downame, *The Christian Warfare* (London: Printed by William Standsby, 1634), 259. Downame (1571–1652) was a Church of England clergyman.

10. Nicholas Bownd, *Sabbathum Veteris et Noui Testamenti* (London: By Felix Kyngston, 1606), 394.

11. Thomas Watson, *Heaven Taken by Storm* (London: Printed by R.W., 1670), 73.

12. John Bunyan, *Grace Abounding to the Chief of Sinners* (London: Printed by George Larkin, 1666), 10.

13. Ibid., 11.

14. Jonathan Michel, A Discourse of the Glory to Which God Hath Called Believers by Jesus Christ (London: Printed for Nathaniel Ponder, 1677), 1–2.

15. Miller McPherson and Lynn Smith-Lovin, "Social Isolation in America: Change in Core Discussion Networks over Two Decades," *American Sociological Review* 71, no. 3 (June 2006): 353–54.

16. Dallas Willard, "The Reality of the Spiritual Life," Christian Spirituality and Soul Care Lecture Series, Talbot School of Theology, Biola University, La Mirada, CA, Fall 2006.

Chapter 9: Biblical Hospitality

1. Parker Palmer, *The Company of Strangers: Christians and the Renewal of America's Public Life* (New York: Crossroad, 1981), 69.

Chapter 10: Biblical Thanksgiving

1. C. S. Lewis and Don Giovanni Calabria, *The Latin Letters of C. S. Lewis*, trans. and ed. Martin Moynihan (South Bend, IN: St. Augustine's Press, 1998), 49.

2. Robert A. Emmons and Michael E. McCullough, "Counting Blessings

Versus Burdens: An Experimental Investigation of Gratitude and Subjective Well-Being in Daily Life," *Journal of Personality and Social Psychology*, 2003, Vol. 84, No. 2, 377–89.

3. P. C. Craigie, "Mercy" in *The Evangelical Dictionary of Theology*, ed. Walter A. Elwell (Grand Rapids: Baker Books, 1984).

4. Richard Greenham, *The Workes of the Reverend and Faithfull Servant of Jesus Christ M. Richard Greenham* (London: Imprinted by Felix Kingston, 1599), "388" (pagination error in original document).

ALSO AVAILABLE

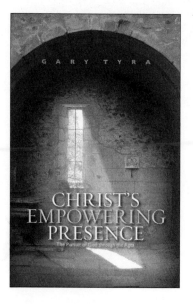

We all have deep longings that can be filled only by Christ's empowering presence, but we struggle with that becoming a reality. *Christ's Empowering Presence* claims that the cultivation of an ongoing awareness of Christ's presence in our lives is at the heart of the Christian experience and provides the reader with:

• A clear vision of what the experience of Christ's empowering presence looks like
• Citations from the spiritual masters that will inspire readers to intend to live the rest of their lives enjoying Christ's empowering presence
• A thoughtful discussion of the means by which this key spiritual dynamic can be experienced on a moment-by-moment basis.

Paperback, 223 pages, 5.5 x 8.5
ISBN: 978-1-60657-096-8
Retail: $15.99

Available for purchase at book retailers everywhere.

Christians who think simplistically often imagine sin is a problem only for unbelievers, yet reality clearly points to its looming presence in our lives and its deadly impact on the church. By not openly admitting and addressing the sin in our lives, we deceive ourselves; and the world looking on is misled through this hypocrisy. *Spiritual Formation* is a scalpel to cut away tumors of ignorance, avoidance, and pride, creating honest believers who then will be an authentic witness to a hurting world.

Paperback, 224 pages, 6 x 9
ISBN: 978-1-93406-882-3
Retail: $19.99

Available for purchase at book retailers everywhere.